CW00363039

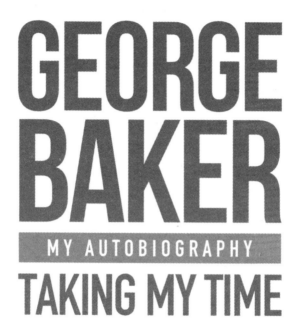

GEORGE BAKER

MY AUTOBIOGRAPHY

TAKING MY TIME

RACING POST

For Isabella
I did this for you so one day you can read what your
Dad did for a living in an earlier phase of his life.

Copyright © George Baker and Tom Peacock 2018

The right of George Baker and Tom Peacock to be identified as the authors of this work has been asserted by them in accordance with the Copyright, Designs and Patents Act 1988.

First published in Great Britain in 2018 by
Racing Post Books
27 Kingfisher Court, Hambridge Road, Newbury, Berkshire, RG14 5SJ

10 9 8 7 6 5 4 3 2 1

All rights reserved. No part of this publication may be reproduced, stored in a retrieval system, or transmitted in any form or by any means, electronic, mechanical, photocopying, recording, or otherwise, without the prior written permission of the publishers.

A catalogue record for this book is available from the British Library.

ISBN 978-1-910497-89-0

Designed by Fiona Pike
Cover designed by Jay Vincent

Printed and bound in the UK by CPI Group (UK) Ltd, Croydon, CR0 4YY
Every effort has been made to fulfil requirements with regard to copyright material. The author and publisher will be glad to rectify any omissions at the earliest opportunity.

www.racingpost.com/shop

CONTENTS

FOREWORD

I've known George ever since I began my career. He was riding regularly for my dad's stable from the very early days and the fact that he continued to do so right up until he was forced to retire should tell you everything you need to know about the regard in which we all hold him.

George had every attribute that you would look for in a top jockey. He had great hands, balance, judgement and intelligence, and deserved all of the success he had, from his Group One wins in France, Britain and Ireland, to his victory in the St Leger.

Having to keep a close eye on your weight is part and parcel of the life of everyone in our profession but what George had to deal with is very unusual. I would say that there are only three or four others on the circuit of a similar size to him who have to demonstrate such incredible discipline. His management of it was exceptional, from maintaining his fitness and looking after his diet to simply being sensible.

There's also another side to George, which is his dark sense of humour. You'd see it in the weighing room every day, and hopefully that comes across through the pages of this book. He's a realistic, serious guy in many ways, but he has always been very dry and very amusing.

All jockeys are only too aware that we are involved in a dangerous sport and that accidents can happen, but that didn't make it any easier to take when we heard the news of what had happened to George in Switzerland. The reality is that the racing world continues and everyone gets on with things, as George would know only too well, but that didn't mean that we weren't all very worried about him. He couldn't have too many visitors in hospital to start with and when I first spoke with him on the phone in around April or May, just a few weeks after his accident, I could tell that he still had a long way to go in his recovery. Happily, he has continued to make fantastic progress and is now able to lead a normal life again.

You don't get any of the airy-fairy stuff with George, no nonsense at all, and he has been like this throughout our friendship. I admired him as a rider, and I continue to admire him as a person.

Ryan Moore

PROLOGUE

It was the end of February 2017 and I was lying battered, bruised and not making very much sense in a hospital bed in Switzerland.

'How are you feeling?' asked the nurse.

'Aren't I doing well?' I managed to mumble as I drifted in and out of consciousness. 'Time's a massive healer.'

It had been one day since the accident which was going to alter my life forever, and the first time I had actually spoken to anyone.

I'm not quite sure what I would have meant by time being a healer. It's unlikely that I had already rediscovered the art of sarcasm after suffering a highly traumatic brain injury. Certainly my behaviour over the next few days would suggest that this definitely wasn't the case. I was to be deadly serious about everything, including my intention to defy mental and physical impossibilities and return to my job as a jockey as soon as possible.

Most probably I was just talking rubbish to the nurse, but at least for my wife Nicola, who had flown to my bedside in the Alps as soon as she had received the news of my high-speed fall in a horserace on the ice in St Moritz, it was a rare moment of light relief.

Nicola would need a sense of humour, not to mention untold resilience. We had a four-month baby daughter at home and her husband had become a very different man in the 40 or so hours since she had last seen him. One whom many thought would have difficulty leading a normal life again.

When I was first approached by the *Racing Post* about telling my story, I thought, 'No way'. I didn't think I had anything particularly interesting to write about, and couldn't think of anything worse than trawling back through my past. I'm a positive thinker and I prefer to concentrate on the future. I suppose it didn't seem interesting to me because I'd done it.

I had actually put the letter away somewhere, before Nicola found it and urged me to think again. She reminded me that I'd spent two months in hospital, firstly with severe memory loss and behavioural changes, and later teaching myself to walk again and fend for myself. At different stages of my recovery I've been confused, depressed, upset, angry and terrified but somehow always managed to drive myself onwards.

I also had a lot to tell about defying physical boundaries to become a top-class Flat rider who collected 1,364 winners during a career lasting more than 17 years. Not only did I win the St Leger, the oldest of the sport's five 'Classics', but I reached a century of winners during the Turf season. That is an achievement only a handful of riders will reach, and one which my agent, Guy Jewell, and I were particularly proud of.

And I managed all of this despite being 5ft 11in – as tall as any other jockey in a weighing room dominated by those who are much smaller. I had restricted my weight to only 9st, when naturally I would be perhaps 3st heavier. Nearly every single day that I was riding, which was most days, I would have to lose between 3 and 4lb, by jumping in a bath for an hour and sweating. When you say that to a normal person, they just can't get their head around it. When I look at a recent picture of myself, John Francome, Carl Llewellyn and AP McCoy, and see that I was the tallest and at 11st 7lb nearly the heaviest, I can't get my head around it myself.

Nicola really won me over when she told me that our daughter Bella had never seen me ride, aside from one time when she was only about a week old. It flicked a switch inside: I realised I would like her to know what her father once did for a living, and what he went through later in his life.

Not only did we also come to the conclusion that my experiences might provide some help to those who find themselves in similar positions, but we thought it would be a great way to put an end to this phase of my life. You will find I have been truthful the whole way, though, because I haven't got anything to hide, and I don't have any regrets.

CHAPTER ONE
A BRIGHT FUTURE

Looking back I feel sorry for Mr Rasman. For he was my teacher and had called me into his office at secondary school for one of those 'What do you want to do when you grow up?'-type career-advisory meetings. 'Being a jockey' would definitely not be the right answer.

When I told him my plan, he just said, 'You've got to think of doing something else.' He gave me a lecture about it being like saying I wanted to be a professional footballer, that only so many people made the grade, and did I realise that further education and staying on for sixth form would be beneficial for my future?

I wasn't cheeky to him, but he could have sat there for two hours. 'You're talking to the wrong person,' I was just thinking. 'I'm going to be a jockey, and I don't care what you tell me.' I don't know whether my mindset would have allowed me to think otherwise: I was properly obsessed.

My mother discovered I had written much the same in the form you were required to fill in about careers. Jockey first, racehorse trainer second – 'although it would be very hard to get into' – and farrier as 'a last resort'.

My parents, Peter and Tracie, would have known my intentions for years. My dad would have loved to be a jockey himself, but after spending some time running a stud and even a spell as a policeman, he has been a farrier for more than half his life. Dad has rarely strayed beyond the triangle of Wiltshire, Berkshire and Hampshire, and used to be in the service of many of the top stables in Lambourn. He shod Burrough Hill Lad and Corbiere, who won the Cheltenham Gold Cup and the Grand National respectively for Jenny Pitman in the early 1980s, and countless other great horses from the area.

We never moved far from what is Britain's second most important training centre after Newmarket. I was born on 1 September 1982 at Savernake Hospital in the Wiltshire town of Marlborough, and shortly afterwards we moved to Lambourn. I don't think it was ever Mum's cup of tea, as it can be quite busy for such a small place. One Sunday she had taken me out in the buggy down the high street and someone driving a car had spotted two lads they knew just in front of us. Suddenly the driver had swerved off the road and was coming straight towards us at speed, avoiding Mum and me by a matter of feet. From that moment onwards, Mum decided that she could no longer face living there.

So we relocated a few miles away to Aldbourne, a more peaceful and sleepy kind of village with just a post office, a small shop, a library and a few pubs. My time at St. Michael's primary school would not be one of my 'Mastermind' subjects, but I remember having what was probably a fairly standard childhood, with games of football on the playing field at the back of the house with all the other kids who lived in Whitley Road.

I was the oldest of four children. My two sisters, Zoe and Scarlett, came in between, and my brother Zac arrived quite a long time after the rest of us. Scarlett works for a problem-solving company near Birmingham which makes parts for aero engines. I'd say she was the most intelligent of us all, and she has done really well with her career. Zoe is a nanny, an absolute star, with two children of her own now, who lives on the outskirts of south London. Both my sisters liked doing the pony stuff during primary school, but when it got a bit more serious and they had to make a decision about taking it further than going to gymkhanas, they lost interest.

Zac, who is 12 years younger than me, was never as keen on riding as I was until he was 14 or 15, but has enjoyed some success as an amateur over jumps. We have two key things in common. Large noses and long legs. If you've seen me and think I was big for a jockey, you want to take a look at Zac, who at 6ft 2in towers over me. We do keep in touch, but there's quite an age gap between us, and Zac was still very small by the time I left home. Hopefully we can become a bit closer and I can help him out a bit more, but he's happy and needs to row his own boat. I love watching him ride – he's always prepared to take his time on horses, and gets them into a fantastic rhythm, which is something I like to think I used to be fairly decent at myself.

I think Zac's bottom weight is 10st 8lb or 10st 9lb, so if he'd ever wanted to ride on the Flat, he'd have had to cut a leg off. His world has been tougher than mine, not only with the regular falls, but also because there seem to be so few spare rides going around in jumping compared with the Flat. I'm glad he's enjoying what he's doing, and he had a good run in point-to-pointing, but it's harder for him to start earning a proper living and planning for the future.

Although as a family we've always all got on fairly well, it's been a strange symptom of what I call the 'racing bubble' that at times you forget what's going on in the real world. In a weird way, when I was flat out in my riding career, family maybe took a bit of a back seat. We'd see each other at family gatherings, but Christmas would come around and we'd hardly remember another time in the whole year when we'd all got together. You always say you'll make more of an effort during the next few months, but it never really happens. I do regret the lack of time I've spent with them, but a positive effect of my accident has been to bring us closer together again. I wish they all lived a bit closer to me, but everyone has to get on with their own lives, don't they?

I must have inherited my affinity for horses from Dad, who is masterful around them. Being a farrier is a matter of being on the ball: he's very calm and aware of where you can and can't stand around a horse, and knows that the majority of them don't want to help you out when you're trimming their hooves and fitting new shoes. More recently he has mainly concentrated on his work at the local racecourses such as Newbury, Kempton and Sandown, being on standby if any of the runners have problems with their feet. His expertise was even called upon for perhaps the most famous performer of them all, Frankel, before Sir Henry Cecil's superstar ran in the Lockinge Stakes at Newbury.

The apple of my dad's eye, though, was always Ra Nova, who won what used to be known as the Schweppes Gold Trophy at Newbury in 1984 for the local trainer Nan Kennedy. There is a photograph of me somewhere, aged only about two, proudly holding Ra Nova, and it is quite significant because it was taken by Jay Boyd Kirkman, the American equestrian artist. Dad had been shoeing Ra Nova and Mr Kirkman, who at the time was just a humble art student, had been practising his craft in Nan Kennedy's yard. He had drawn a pencil sketch of Dad at work, which his dad still has, and quickly took a photo with me holding Ra Nova's head for reference purposes. Dad was always meaning to commission him to paint it, but unfortunately Mr Kirkman's profile suddenly rose sharply and his work became rather out of Dad's price range.

Because I was introduced to horses at such a young age, I was fearless around them. I'd be taken around all the yards and, as I saw Dad underneath a horse shoeing him, it must have seemed a very natural instinct for me to just walk into the stable and grab the poor horse by its tail. It would give Dad, who was obviously concentrating on what is a dangerous job, quite a fright. While Nan Kennedy's experienced jumpers would not bat an eyelid if a child came in to play with them, it could have been a very different matter with one of the flighty two-year-olds from other yards. When I was a few years older,

I graduated to the very important job of being Dad's 'chief horse holder', as often in the very small yards there was no one else around to help out.

As I've said though, I was going to be a jockey and didn't waste any time before riding horses myself, being taught first by Mandy Moody at the Lambourn Riding School, and then by Sarah West in Aldbourne. My parents are pretty sure that even then, as I sat on the ponies with my knees up, I was going to be a jockey. When Dad was sitting watching the racing on the television in the afternoons, a small figure would suddenly appear alongside him and put his tiny saddle on the arm of the sofa. Unlike some aspiring young jockeys, I was never Lester Piggott, or another famous name, and as I rode that sofa leg, I was always going to be just me, George Baker.

I think the seed of a career in riding was really planted when Dad was working at Newbury races and I'd be taken along. While he was busy I would just stand watching the horses going around the parade ring. I don't think I was obsessed with the racing itself: I just remember being absolutely fascinated by the horses and the jockeys.

By something of a twist of fate, I was lucky enough to be given a horse of my own: Copper, a 13-hands chestnut pony who otherwise was probably going to be put down. He lived at Sarah West's yard, but the people who owned him had told Sarah that he didn't suit their children, and when they returned from their holidays they didn't want to see him again. I think Dad gave them £200 to get him out of the way.

Our problems started with him almost immediately as the little bugger proved to be a devil to catch. You'd go out to him with food in your hand, and he'd wait until you almost had him and would then do a smart 360 and piss off. We finally nailed it, after a good few months of sweat and swearing, by leaving a piece of rope on his head collar.

In times gone by, Copper had been a good jumping pony, but now he'd become a bit of a lunatic. He could be very fresh and do some weird things, and was basically not a very nice ride. He also had just the two gears – slow and fast. But I loved him.

I'd be pretty fearless on him, and used to fall off quite a bit – but when he wanted to jump he was absolutely brilliant. Rather than being one of those ponies who would just plod along and teach you nothing, Copper had a soft mouth and would wave his head around, basically the perfect introduction to what it would be like to ride fully-grown and challenging racehorses.

He was really like a miniature thoroughbred, a pocket rocket. It's just a shame that back then there wasn't the organised pony racing we have these days, as he'd have been an absolute wizard at it. We did a bit of the pony club stuff, mainly showjumping and quite a bit of cross-country but I didn't have much time for the dressage. We both wanted to go fast and neither of us, particularly me, had the patience for trotting around in circles when we could be flat out winning imaginary races.

I was already riding racehorses by the time I was a teenager, and there weren't enough hours in the day to do everything. Once in a while Copper and I would go to a horse show, and on one occasion at Stonar School, which has a well-respected equestrian centre, we managed to beat adult showjumpers in several competitions. We even went to the Beaufort Hunter Trials, which are held at the same places as the Badminton Horse Trials, and we jumped three or four full-size steeplechase fences before I pulled Copper up. For some reason, then as later in my career, I had no desire to be a jump jockey and had zero interest in jumping fences. I liked going fast but didn't want to get hurt!

I owed Copper a lot in my riding development, and he was able to have a long and happy retirement, right up to when I met Nicola in my mid-20s. When he was a very old boy her mum ended up keeping an eye on him.

In the sense of having my own pony I suppose I had a fairly privileged upbringing, but we were more what you would describe as a proper, hard-working family, and as Dad was so busy, rarely having even a day off, there might only be the odd holiday to Cornwall. We certainly didn't go abroad all the time. Mum has worked in schools and now helps Dad to run the farriery business, but in those days it was a full-time job looking after the rest of the Baker family. She is extremely caring, and as she raced around everywhere as our taxi driver nothing was ever too much to ask.

I wouldn't describe myself as the greatest student, even within my own family, although I wasn't too bad. At primary school I suffered quite badly with dyslexia, which was probably not recognised then as widely as it is nowadays, and I was taken off for specialist tutoring sessions in Swindon. I've always struggled with spelling, but instead of blaming it on dyslexia, more often than not I just felt I wasn't very bright. The days of predictive texting were yet to come, and were very welcomed by George Baker when they did!

I really loved my secondary school at Park House, mainly because there was a particular emphasis on sports. Park House is in Newbury, well outside what should have been my catchment area, but Dad used to work for a lady called Heather White, who was a sports teacher at the school and had some horses just outside Aldbourne. Somehow they swung it to get me admitted. It's quite a drive to Newbury from Aldbourne, and Heather would give me a lift every day.

I was a decent long-distance runner, reaching county level at cross-country. I also played a fair bit of rugby, captaining my house under the tutelage of Stefan Czerpak, something of a local legend who ended up coaching at England youth level before his sadly premature death in 1998.

Believe it or not, at that stage I was tiny – 6st 10lb by the time I left. There's a very embarrassing picture of me in the rugby team, on the end of the row next to all of these giant lads, and it looks as if my picture's been superimposed. I was so small that occasionally when I was tackled I would dislocate my left shoulder, only to pop it back in and keep going.

Being born in September, I was the oldest in my year at school, so it came around quite quickly that at the age of 16 I could get a moped. I could spend the early morning at the racing stables a few miles away in Kingston Lisle, and then head on to Park House for lessons. I must have spent hours on that moped, chugging through the foulest of weather. I thought I was a right boy racer, but on the dangerous A4 from Hungerford to Newbury, when you can only reach 30mph you're even getting overtaken by the lorries, so I used to skip along the back roads and it made no difference in time. It could be pretty unpleasant in the winter, and it got so cold on the moped that I would have to stop it in Baydon, around ten minutes from Aldbourne, have a little run around to warm up, and then have to do the same thing when I reached Lambourn.

I fell off it once, and still don't know what on earth happened. Going along the Wantage Road, just out of Lambourn, I somehow fell asleep and went over the verge. I'm still surprised how completely unharmed I was – I suppose it helps that when you fall asleep you're fairly relaxed – but the moped had done a bit of damage. To my horror I discovered it had made a fair mess of the fence next to the trainer Willie Muir's stable. I wasn't about to get a serious telling-off, or foot an expensive bill for some repairs, so I just got back on and rode off. To this day, I've not told Willie about it. I even rode a winner for him in my first full season, so hopefully he'll forgive me now!

It seems strange that everyone at school apart from Mr Rasman seemed to know about my riding ambitions, as I was spending every spare moment with horses. Even my wonderful headmaster, Derek Greenup, would say, 'Just go, enjoy yourself,' and let me bunk off to the races whenever there was a meeting at Newbury on a Friday afternoon, and on Monday nights I could sometimes be found waiting outside school for a lift down to Windsor races.

I'm not sure they make teachers like Mr Greenup any more. He could see I really wanted to make it as a jockey, and I believe he had been similarly liberal with pupils who had other non-educational passions. I certainly wasn't the most intelligent person at school when it came to exams and schoolwork, but as long as I was good during class he trusted me to do near enough what I wanted. I suspect he quietly liked racing, and my parents, who stayed in touch with him, tell me he followed my career with interest. He was an absolute gentleman.

Probably the one thing Mr Greenup would have frowned upon was my attitude to my GCSEs, and hopefully now that we are more than 20 years down the line I will be able to get away with something of a white lie.

I had enrolled at the Northern Racing College at Doncaster to do my apprentice course, and it turned out that in order to complete it, I would have to miss my final GCSE in English. Given the amount I must have talked about horses, and all the hours they spent driving me to events and the stables – I would never stay in bed and not want to go riding – I'm sure Mum and Dad were kind of resigned to racing being my chosen pursuit. I was in such a rush to get going that the thought of waiting another six months for the next apprentice course just didn't seem bearable, and so Mum and I kind of decided together that I would go to Doncaster instead. On the day of the exam there was a phone call from the school asking where I was, but my complicit Mum, bless her, was unable to pick up at that time, so the answerphone got the bollocking.

My time at the Northern Racing College was a really good laugh. It was basically all young lads, 16-year-olds, staying away from home for the first time. Mark Usher, who was going to employ me, had written a letter to the college outlining how much experience I had, so I was fast-tracked and didn't have to do another nine-week course to learn basic horse management. All I had was a week's apprentice course, mainly learning some rules, doing a bit on the equicizer (a mechanical horse), proving my fitness and receiving a bit of coaching, and I was away.

A handful of us made it to riding in races. Mickey Doyle rode for Andrew Balding and in 2001 very nearly won the Cesarewitch aboard Palua, whilst Adam Hawkins had a go first on the Flat and then over jumps for a few years, and married Steph Hollinshead, the Staffordshire trainer. The best known of them would be Dave Allan, who came along as steadily as I did and in recent years has done even better, riding a heap of Classic winners in India and having a good link with Tim Easterby in the north of England.

We actually stayed in a hotel in Doncaster rather than at the college itself and, surprisingly I suppose, we weren't really supervised at all. We were dropped back at the hotel at about five o'clock and given an allowance for dinner and the evening to ourselves. Of course, we went and ate absolute rubbish and attempted to go into all the pubs, only to be ID'd everywhere and turned away. I think we still thought that we were out living the life, even if we were probably fairly tame.

There was a bit of a surprise on the second-last evening, when the instructors told us there was going to be a weigh-in the next day.

After eating a week's worth of junk food, all of us bricked it, even though with hindsight it wasn't particularly important. I suppose it was just for official purposes, and that the trainers many of us were about to go to work for would not want to discover we were now much heavier than we were supposed to be.

Adam, who was quite a big lad, was the most worried of all, and I remember that evening we all went off running to try to burn off some of those excess calories. But it turned out there had been no need for all the panic, as we all passed.

It was good getting to know new people and it felt like we were all in it together, but it did make me realise how competitive it was out there. I had been rather protected up to this point and was now going to have to face competition from so many jockeys wanting to make it.

I left school on the Friday, started working for Mark Usher full-time on the Monday, and had my first ride that week. The report from the Northern Racing College, that my Mum still treasures, read 'This lad could have a bright future'.

CHAPTER TWO
WORK EXPERIENCE

When little George Baker first started spending weekends away riding out in a racing stable he was smaller, younger and definitely more naïve than most aspiring jockeys. And he was only 12.

Yet at that age I was already allowed to spend weekends and school holidays with an Irishman called Dermid Hyde, who was one of Dad's clients and had a small yard in Membury, close to where you get off the M4 to reach Lambourn.

Dermid was a cheerful and amusing guy, a bit of a one-off who had ridden a few winners as an amateur for the great Toby Balding, but seemed to struggle along as a trainer. He only had about ten horses, mainly moderate jumpers and a couple of Flat horses, and apart from his brother Mark, who dealt with the yard work, he had no staff at all and basically did everything himself, including riding them all out.

Times must have been quite hard for Dermid, not that I noticed at such a young age, and I don't think he even trained a winner during the time I was with him. Certainly I never questioned why he would always pick me up at just after 5 a.m. on Sundays, or why none of the horses would have any sheets with their names on when we rode down the lethal hill into Lambourn. It only occurred to me much later on that he clearly wasn't paying any fees, and was using the gallops before anyone else was up and about!

Later on, when Dermid and Mark moved to a little village near Marlborough, we would sneak over and use the famous Manton gallops in a similar way. It must have been quite handy for him having a young lad coming in and working for nothing, but I don't want to paint a poor picture of Dermid. He was an incredible grafter, working his arse off with a tiny string and trying to make it pay, but also a really kind man who pretty much taught me to ride racehorses. I'd sit on most of the horses in the yard, learned to ride short and got used to a racing saddle. He also started me on the road to the two most important lessons of all – judging pace and settling a horse by having 'good hands'. I was so small and weak when I started going into Dermid's that horses would bolt with me all the time. I'd usually be following Dermid up the gallops, doing a normal canter and trying to sit a couple of lengths behind him. But I wouldn't be strong enough to hold the horses back and before too long I'd swoop past and be a couple of furlongs in front of him. You find the horse is suddenly going hell-for-leather and you just have to hope that they're going to pull themselves up by the end of it.

You often see people showing forcefulness with a horse and yanking them in the mouth, but there was only going to be one winner if I started grabbing the reins up short and doing stuff like that. In the early days I wouldn't trust a horse to jump off into a canter with a long enough rein thinking I'd be able to hold it, and a shorter rein would invariably make them keen. I'd have to win the battle with good hands. So with a great deal of help and patience from Dermid, I gained the confidence to trust them with a good length of rein, and to do everything nice and gradually. That way, they'd be more relaxed and in a better frame of mind, and I wouldn't be hanging on for dear life.

I'd even go racing with him and, although I wasn't old enough to have a stable pass, I'd still lead the horse around while he'd go and fetch the saddle. Thinking back, it was probably quite hard work, but I loved it. Copper came to Dermid's second yard, too. He was ridden out every day with the racehorses and must have become seriously fit – yet another reason why I wish there had been some competitive pony racing.

Within a couple of years, Dad had found me another opportunity with Mark Usher, a man I have known for most of my life. Mark is an underrated trainer who was once assistant to the renowned

Henry Candy, and had set up his own business near to his old boss in Kingston Lisle. Although it's not far from Lambourn, Kingston Lisle is its own little community with a few small trainers, and everyone seemed to know each other.

Mark was a great horseman. When you watched him breaking young horses in before they were ready to be trained, he was always so patient. Most of them were badly bred, and sometimes hadn't been well handled when they were young, but the majority of them turned into nice rides because of Mark's expertise. This way of looking after horses fed down to me a little bit, and I have always tried to be kind and understanding with them.

I don't look it now but back then, when I say I was small, I really was. As in five-and-a-bit-stone small at Dermid's. I was big going into Year 7 but tiny when I came out at Year 11 and I don't think I grew at all at secondary school, so it seemed obvious from that age that I wasn't going to be jump jockey material.

From going out in the mornings when it was just Dermid and I chatting away, I was now at a stable with maybe 30 Flat horses, and all the associated banter and mickey-taking that you get with a bunch of other lads. Everyone was kind to me because I was just a kid, but it's a different outlook, and you do start to man up quite quickly. I was a bit quiet, I suppose, and I might have found it harder in an even bigger yard, but I was still quite confident and able to stand up for myself when I needed to.

You wouldn't just ride one or two horses; you'd get plenty of variations, and that's the way you improve. Jeff Marshall, who used to ride in the north for Mick Easterby, was there, and Mark's apprentice at the time was Wayne Hutchinson, who has since become a top-class jump jockey.

Wayne is a little older than me, but we became good friends, and were both there because we wanted to improve. He's a lovely, quiet rider to watch: he lets things happen, and I think he would have done all right on the Flat, but it soon became quite apparent that he was getting quite big.

My arrival probably meant he was shoved out of the door a bit more quickly than he would have wanted, and he moved on to the likes of Stan Mellor and Jeff King, who taught him his trade over fences. Wayne has ended up having a long career over jumps with Alan King and, without being disrespectful, he has only really been held back by having a lot of injuries from falls which have caused him to miss out on good rides.

At first, my parents took me to Mark's for weekends and holidays, but having the moped allowed me more independence and I could ride there more frequently. I'm sure I wasn't supposed to be there as often as I was, but it was probably hard to stop me. Sometimes in the afternoons I would just be sitting in the tack room killing time, as the yard was the only place I really wanted to be. So, I would take my riding out saddle into the barn, tack up a few bales of shavings and using the glass windows as mirrors, I'd practice riding George Baker-style finishes. Jane Whitfield (now Tuddenham), who worked for Mark, would take pity on me and take me into her house and make me lunch.

In my last year at school – when you are supposed to go somewhere to do work experience – I asked if I could go to Mark's and get another week of riding out. For some reason, unfortunately, this wasn't allowed, because I had already been there, so my uncle Jerry, who is also a farrier, asked the trainer Peter Makin, who was based at Ogbourne Maizey just outside Marlborough, if I could come and ride out for him for the week instead.

The week was a complete revelation. Kingston Lisle is quite small and, whilst Mark wasn't doing badly, Peter would have had about double the amount of horses. Back then he had all those good sprinters like Imperial Beauty, who won the Prix de l'Abbaye. It really opened my eyes as to what the bigger yards were about.

You're fearless when you're a teenager, but sometimes you get a wake-up call. Out on my own one Sunday morning at Mark's, I had given a canter to a horse who had come from a point-to-point yard. She had been quite fresh and, for reasons known only to her, when we had come off the gallops she started bolting down the Blowing Stone Hill towards the crossroads in Kingston Lisle.

That hill is like a ski slope so I realised that if a car happened to hit me, I was dead, and since I couldn't stop her from bolting, I had no option but to bail out by hurling myself over the side. Luckily I had a soft fall by landing in a gorse hedge, picked a few thorns out and headed back to the yard. I could see a few scuff marks where the horse had gone around a corner, but she had happily made her own way back to her stable with not a mark on her.

In retrospect it was quite scary, and for the first time it made me think that what I was doing was actually quite dangerous. If it happened to me now, I'd be in pieces, but when you're young, you just bounce off the ground. All I wanted to do was get back to the yard to see if the horse was all right.

Despite the odd mishap such as this, I had clearly impressed Mark enough for him to take me on full-time after I left school. Then, literally a few days later, on 22 June, 1999, in the Lingfield Loyalty Cards Apprentices' Handicap, he gave me my first ride in public. I was only 16 years old and could already call myself a proper jockey!

Whereas most aspiring riders would expect to keep their heads down and work away as stable staff for many weeks and months before they are finally given their big chance to shine, mine was sort of sprung upon me. Nowadays, with the development of a pony racing scene, some youngsters might have had a few hundred rides before they enter grown-up racing. I'd had one sort-of public ride in a hunt scurry at a point-to-point, but at least I had the advantage of having ridden horses for a long time. This was the opportunity I had been waiting for and I was excited to take this first step into the unknown.

Indian Flag, an ordinary sort of filly, was owned by a lady called Heidi Sweeting, who later in my apprentice life employed Mark as a salaried trainer at her base at White Barn Farm in Lockeridge. I think Mark had been discussing who might ride her in this race with Heidi and her husband Paul, and they had been keen to give me a go, but it had all been a bit of a rush to get all the paperwork through.

The hours ticked by. My parents took me into Wicks' saddlers in Lambourn and bought all of my kit the day before and, as much as I was really excited about the ride, I'll never forget walking into Lingfield that day and absolutely bricking it. As if it wasn't enough that I was a newcomer, Richard Perham was presenting the Racing Channel television station that day and he knew me. The cameras seemed to be on me everywhere, from walking into the paddock to cantering to the start, with Richard explaining how I'd got into the sport and telling all of the viewers that I was a good lad.

After being bigged up so much, luckily I didn't look too bad, and my being so small probably meant that my style looked a bit tidier than it actually was. I held Indian Flag up at the back of the field, took my time and eventually finished third, only beaten two lengths, although I also got cautioned for careless riding! But the race itself was a bit of a blur, and when I got home that day, I wondered what had just happened.

What imprints itself far more strongly is the experience of going into a weighing room for the first time. You've wanted to be a jockey for so long, but you are shoved into a new situation that you've never even thought about. I'd been brought up in a village and was hardly very worldly, and suddenly here I was, surrounded by real-life jockeys. I couldn't tell you which other jockeys were there that day but my most memorable moment was meeting my valet, Brian Yorke, who was to become a guiding figure in this next phase of my career.

Valets are assigned to look after your gear and are the heroes behind the scenes who take a lot of the stress on race day, and I'm not sure all racegoers would even know they are there. They organise everything and are invariably good fun characters. I think they have to be, because they put up with a lot of nonsense from the jockeys. Brian would have me on his books from start to finish, and I would see him almost every day of my working life. He was one of the most senior valets, from several generations of family members in the business, and a proper old-school operator. Pretty soon you would know the script fairly well: to be tidy and respect your gear. He wouldn't need to tell you twice – he just had that sort of air of respect and authority.

Brian was also a mentor to me, and someone to confide in. If you were doing something stupid, or getting wound up, he'd just quietly appear beside you and tell you to calm down. When you're a boy going into a proper man's world, with jockeys I'd watched ride since I was young, you need guidance from people like Brian. It's not that everyone isn't friendly – they are – but when I had become an established jockey I would always try to go over and say hello to a new face, because you do feel very inferior when you're starting out.

The weighing room is like a safe haven for most jockeys, the place to gather your thoughts away from the cameras, but there's a structure and you have to fit in. It's a dangerous sport, and if you're acting like a bit of a dickhead, you don't get on well. I've seen lads come along who think they're the dog's and try to do it their own way, but eventually they all conform to the weighing-room way of doing things, where we all look after one another. They get a wake-up call quite quickly. As lads get more confident, it takes a bit longer to break them down and for the really cocky ones to conform.

Oisin Murphy would be a good example. He came along and was a very talented rider, very confident in his ability and a good talker. I suspect he thought he knew it all, and he had to realise that it's far better to get on with people you're riding against. Say someone is riding in a big race and needs a bit of help, or a bit of room to give their horse the best chance of winning: if you knew your horse was starting to go backwards you would try to help them. You aren't going to go out of your way, and if you're going well you don't give an inch even to your best friend, but what's the point of ruining someone else's race for no reason?

You only have to look at how Oisin has matured and grown up over later years as proof that he has adapted. He was taught well by trainer Andrew Balding, and landed a job as retained jockey for Sheikh Fahad Al Thani's Qatar Racing. I imagine he'll remain at the top for many years.

As much as I got a massive kick out of riding Indian Flag, when it had sunk in by the next day, all I wanted was to do it again. Fortunately Mark had quite a few horses that were suitable for an apprentice, and some other trainers, such as his next-door-neighbour Martin Bosley, helped me out with a few early on.

I needed that winner, though, and it took more than five months and almost 30 rides before I got there. That restlessness of youth crept in: Mark remembers driving back with me from Southwell one day, telling me something about jockeyship after another losing ride, and me slamming my hands down in front of me in frustration. He could tell then that I wanted it very badly.

Finally, one Saturday evening at Wolverhampton in early December, I got there. Beauchamp Magic, who was bred by the well-known owner Erik Penser, came into Mark's yard to be tried as a jumper, but proved to be useless at that, and had quickly established a reputation for being quite quirky. In fact, I'd describe him as an absolute bastard. I reckon he'd drop you twice a week, but you couldn't fall out with him: if you tried to tell him off, he'd go and drop you again. To give him some credit, he brought my riding along at home, he was that tricky, and we had something of a love-hate relationship.

Beauchamp Magic did have some relatively good form during his time with John Dunlop, and had the ability to win races – he was just one of those horses that didn't like being knocked around or told what to do, so having a weak 7lb claimer on his back probably suited him.

I went racing in the horsebox and actually got him ready myself, went back to the weighing room, weighed out and saddled him up. Mark's stepson Lee Newnes, who'd once been a jockey himself, then led him round in the paddock. Although we were a 40-1 chance, I remember feeling very confident, and even told Martin Bosley's dad John, who often drove me to the races, that he should have a few quid on him at 100-1 on the Tote.

During the race, I was off the bridle and pushing Beauchamp Magic along from some way out, but actually he probably just wasn't helping me out much. Luckily the race was over two miles, and when he started passing horses, he began to to travel better. I don't think that my input made much of a difference to him, but I kidded him along and we eventually won quite nicely. Not only that time, either: the following year, as his confidence increased and he worked out how to do things, we won a heap more races.

Winning a race was such a massive buzz. It was not exactly the Cheltenham Festival, when you hear that roar from the punters as the winner goes back down the walkway, and I was covered in muck from the all-weather surface, but I don't think you could pay money to feel how I felt that day. It was only a poxy race at Wolverhampton, but it felt like I'd won the Derby.

Strangely, though, all that was going through my mind soon after it happened, and later as I went back out to lead the horse around to cool off in the racecourse stables, was, 'I want that feeling again.' I wasn't thinking about how amazing it was; I just wanted more winners. I wanted this to be my life and I craved more of that feeling. It was very much like when you hear the legendary AP McCoy talking about how he only wanted to win time after time – that realisation that success is everything.

John Bosley was pretty pleased too – he had won a right few quid from his bet – and it had given Mark a rare cross-card double, as one of his hurdlers had taken the first race at Towcester that afternoon.

It got me my first bit of press in the next day's *Racing Post*, where I had said very maturely, 'I always wanted to be a jockey, and I'm very grateful to Mr Usher for giving me the chance. Beauchamp Magic had been going very well at home and enjoys the all-weather, so I thought he had a chance, and to have won is just brilliant.'

We ended up having some drinks at the races and John drove me back, stopping off at his house in Uffington on the way home to watch the replay on the video recorder. A week or so later, in a claiming race at the equally illustrious Southwell racecourse in Nottinghamshire, I picked up my second winner on another of Mark's horses, Bobona.

Beauchamp Magic, who also gave me my 50th career winner, was to have a far more notable moment in the sun himself just a month later with a guy called Jimmy Shoulder. Jimmy was a fascinating guy, who came from a former coal-mining village in Durham, and was an outstanding footballer who played for Sunderland and Scarborough and even went on to coach the Australian national team. He had been doing some work at Swindon Town FC and, as he had been mad about racing since the time his dad was a bookies' runner, he decided to come and learn to ride at Mark's while I was there.

I'm not sure that Jimmy, who was 53 then, had ever ridden a horse before. Although he was a good size and very fit, he wasn't exactly a natural in the saddle, and there were some very amusing moments. Horses can be really mean sometimes and take the mickey out of inexperienced riders. So he got messed about with and run away with on a regular basis.

When you watch racing on the TV, the jockeys make it look so easy and you take it for granted until you have a go yourself, but it was at least in Jimmy's favour that he was willing to listen and learn. He was brilliant fun, and fulfilled his ambition of riding in an amateur riders' race on Beauchamp Magic at Lingfield. It didn't receive the same celebrity coverage as the cyclist Victoria Pendleton when she rode at Cheltenham, but it still attracted quite a bit of publicity in the media.

Things picked up very quickly for me. As I could do stupidly light weights in those days, including an astonishing 7st 3lb on Indian Flag on my first go, I got busier and busier. When you're young and keen, you'll go anywhere for a ride, and whilst I'd be required for Mark when he had runners, he was quite happy for me to spread my wings to grab other opportunities. Bill Heath, who had a connection with the yard and used to advise Mark on doing the form and placing the horses in the right races, was also a particular help, and would sit with me and analyse the races. He was a very good race reader, and it was great to get a neutral's view on what I was doing right and wrong.

From two wins in 38 rides in my first year, I shot up to managing 55 wins from 621 rides in my second, which saw me drop my apprentice claim down from 7lb to 3lb. I was in such demand that one day I had to get up to Haydock on Merseyside at the last minute, but I hadn't started driving yet. One of Mark's responsibilities as my boss was to sort out my travel arrangements, and he discovered that John Reid, one of the very senior jockeys, was going up on a private plane from a tiny airstrip near Childrey, just outside Wantage. It might have sounded a pretty glamorous way to travel, but not when you saw the plane, which was so small it looked as if you could almost pick it up and throw it in the air. Mark had given me a lift to the airstrip, and his face suggested he was pretty delighted there was only just enough room for me to sit behind John.

I don't think I had even been in a plane before, aside from maybe one childhood holiday with my parents, and the journey was as awful as you might imagine. It didn't help that at Haydock you have to come swooping down through the trees to land. I wasn't rushing to get back for the return journey. When John said we would have to leave before the last, otherwise there was a question mark as to whether it was going to be too dark to land the plane, I couldn't take any more. 'You know what, John,' I said as convincingly as I could, 'I've actually made some arrangements to get back already.' I hadn't got any idea how I was going to make it home, but at that moment I would gladly have paid for a taxi all the way back down south. I did manage to cadge a lift back somehow, and getting my driving licence a little while later put an end to any more surprise plane journeys. In later years, I had to man-up about the whole thing as sometimes plane travel is the only way to get to two meetings in one day.

Patrick Haslam in Yorkshire and the Scotsman Jim Goldie were early supporters, as was Mark Brisbourne, who trains in Shropshire, and for whom I built up a good relationship with a consistent low-level handicapper called Adobe. This did mean that when I had my own car I just spent nearly all my time in it, going up to somewhere like Hamilton, coming back home, and the next day motoring off somewhere else in the country.

Patrick Haslam, or 'Mr Haslam' as I would probably have addressed him, was an old-school trainer who wanted everything done in a certain way. I'd describe him as authoritarian rather than particularly warm, and you had to be on your A-game with him. Nevertheless, he was a brilliant trainer, knew all of his horses inside out and what their abilities were. As much as we got on fine, I don't think he'd exactly have wanted me to go for a pint with him, and less so after one particular morning in Middleham.

If I was racing for a couple of days up north, I'd stay with another young jockey, Keith Dalgleish. Keith was based in Middleham with Mark Johnston, and suggested that I rode out for Mark with him, as he was an up-and-coming trainer. It hadn't occurred to me that first I should have been to see Patrick Haslam, given I was riding nearly all of his Flat horses that needed a claiming jockey. On the way to the gallops we passed Paul Mulrennan, who was Mr Haslam's apprentice. 'What are you doing riding out for him?' he asked. As soon as I got off my horse, I looked at my phone and saw I had four missed calls from Patrick Haslam. Paul had dobbed me in and Patrick wasn't very happy. It was quickly established that from then on in the mornings I wouldn't be riding out for Mark anymore.

During those months, Keith and I had fun being irresponsible young lads. Neither of us had weight problems, and coming back from the races we would usually stop at McDonalds or similar and eat junk food all the time. It's weird how things go, though. The next thing you know, Keith had to pack up because he became too big (subsequently becoming a successful trainer) and I entered the second phase of my career that was to be dictated throughout by my battle with the scales.

At that stage I was nowhere near the height I am now. My first growing spurt, from being a midget to about normal Flat jockey size, came during the time I was invited to spend a couple of months during the winter riding for Godolphin in Dubai, which Mark agreed to as there was a danger I was going to burn through my claim too quickly. Once an apprentice has lost all of their weight allowance, they are a far less valuable commodity to trainers, and it would have been foolish to have wasted mine winning small races on the all-weather. As I pushed my luggage trolley into the airport, my parents remember, it seemed as though it was still taller than me, and when I pushed it out on my return, I was now the taller. They think it was the power of the sun. It's strange – one minute you're fine, then suddenly it was as if both Keith and I had been sleeping in the greenhouse in growbags.

As I was travelling around so much, I got to know lots of different lads pretty well. The racing community is such a small one, you're seeing the same people every day, so friendships are built quickly. We'd share lifts up and down the country, not only to save money but also to cut down on the driving. I remember driving to Musselburgh racecourse in Edinburgh with a load of the southern lads, and stopping off on the way home at a service station, where everyone came back with drinks and milkshakes. Alan Daly was at the wheel, a tough but very amusing guy who would ride here, there and everywhere for the likes of Bill Turner and Marcus Tregoning, and who'd been stable lads' boxing champion something like four years in a row, so not a man to be messed with.

Alan had a sponsored Volkswagen Bora at the time, and he was very proud of his car, so after the others got out I thought I'd be a good lad and pick up all the litter and put it in the bin. However, I must've left a bottle of milkshake, the top was undone, and it spilled on his prized seats. The next day I was at Sandown, just sitting in the weighing room minding my own business, when Alan suddenly rushed up, grabbed me by the throat, and pinned me up against the wall. 'Don't you ever leave any fucking rubbish in my car again!'

Alan was the only jockey I can think of who would have been a match in the ring for Franny Norton, who probably could have turned professional if he hadn't become a jockey. Luckily I was saved a beating, and we ended up becoming very good friends. He ended up retraining as a firefighter.

CHAPTER THREE
AN AGENT FOR CHANGE

Accidents seem to have played a big part in my life so far, and another was to alter my career, my outlook and in particular, my body size.

At Glorious Goodwood in the middle of the summer in 2002, I was due to ride a two-year-old of Mark's called Stagnite in a nursery race. He was generally a straightforward horse, but I remember he was being led around the paddock in a chifney bit, a solid metal ring in the mouth often used for big, strong colts, because they will respect it more than just a head collar. Soon after I had got on him I think the girl leading him up must have caught him in the mouth, and it caused him to rear up. He flipped over, I fell on the floor and he landed on top of me.

I'm very lucky they had just changed the surface on the walkway at Goodwood, and put in some of those square, softer tiles like they have in the paddock. If I had landed on tarmac, it could have been horrible. That said, I think it must have been quite a shock for spectators that afternoon, as I believe they put screens up around me, and it caused a long delay to the race.

I can't recall much about the incident, but I was knocked out for a bit and had to spend a couple of days in hospital. It turned out that I had a very, very small bleed on my brain, and with head injuries you have to take your time to come back. It meant being out of action for about eight months, most of which, luckily, was through the winter when the Flat racing was less important. I had moved out of Aldbourne to live in a place in Swindon I shared with Zoe and David Creech, who worked for Mark, and I couldn't do anything when I was off, aside from some helping out at the yard. The main thing I remember is that I was on medication for three months and wasn't allowed to drink, which is pretty tedious when you're a young lad with a growing social life. I was also temporarily banned from driving. I'm sure I must have been a pain to Zoe, David and my parents throughout the next few weeks and months, but they were good to me. One thing is for certain: after that I never got on a horse with a chifney on – I would always make the lad or lass take it off first.

A lot changed during that period, but the most obvious was my physique. I don't know why, but I just grew. I literally went from 8st 1lb or 2lb to coming back the following spring and wasting my arse off to do 8st 9lb. In effect my natural weight had gone up by at least a stone. I got a few inches taller, too, and my body had gone from being slim and almost feminine-looking before the accident to suddenly filling out.

I hadn't considered mine to have been a particularly bad accident, but when I went to see Dr Michael Turner, the British Horseracing Authority's chief medical adviser, in London for a check-up to find out what I needed to do to be passed fit to ride, he seemed quite shocked that I was all right. Perhaps my medical report had looked more serious than I had realised, or maybe others involved in similar incidents had been a lot worse when they'd come to see him.

Whilst I was given the formal green light to return and could start getting race-fit again, my weight gain was a bit worrying. I do wonder if it was because I'd been so flat-out busy working and riding that I'd actually never given myself the chance to develop. Suddenly stopping and doing nothing had been a trigger. The age of 20 seemed quite old, I thought, to be growing that much.

Although I'm just under six foot, I'd never really thought I was particularly tall, but I remember not long after coming back going into a different yard to ride out and the head lad thinking I was an 'amateur rider', the type of jockey who would usually ride at weights over 10st, rather than an active apprentice at less than 9st.

The trainer Chris Wall, for whom I had started riding occasionally, had kindly said that I could come and see him in Newmarket to help out when I was building towards my comeback. He was fairly amazed to see me looking very different to how I had looked six months earlier. It was as if I'd suddenly gone through puberty – leaving like a boy and coming back a full-grown man.

Whenever taller Flat jockeys come through, people doubt how long they are going to last before they get too heavy for the game and I'm sure many said that about me. It's just like Adam Kirby when he first came into the weighing room. He was quite a big lad but still very light and everyone thought that he would definitely not be around in two years' time. They were wrong about Adam. Not only is he still around, he's doing brilliantly now and riding plenty of Group 1 winners.

Around the same time as I was ready to ride again, Mark had parted ways with Heidi and Paul Sweeting in Lockeridge and had gone training on his own again in Lambourn. It was hard for everyone, and difficult to know what to do. Mark had been my mentor, but he was leaving with a handful of horses, and it was a big ask to expect him to support someone coming back from injury as well. Meanwhile I had moved from Swindon to live with Heidi and Paul, and if I stayed with them, I would be able to ride all of their horses and have a bit more security.

After a discussion with my parents I decided to stay with Heidi and Paul, and the following March they organised me a comeback winner. Soon, though, came a bit of a lull. I was sort of doing OK, fairly busy riding winners here and there, but I was really starting to struggle with my weight. I had an agent called Richard Hunter, who was based up north, and when I was not needed by Heidi and Paul that was where most of my rides were coming from. You shouldn't blame an agent – they are only organising your rides – but my life was involving so much travelling, killing myself to do 8st 9lb to ride pretty ordinary horses, and I was absolutely skint. Don't get me wrong; I enjoyed it for the most part, and it was still a good way of life, but I wasn't happy with just covering my costs.

Some jockeys who got too big to make the weight on the Flat have switched to jumping, but I don't think anyone ever suggested that to my face. Dominic Elsworth did once take me schooling over a few practice obstacles in Lambourn one morning when he was riding for the top jumps trainer Oliver Sherwood. I loved it, if only because it was a change of scenery. As I was schooling alongside Dom, I shouted 'Hup!' every time my horse went to jump, much like you might do with a pony. Dom found it very funny. 'George, the horse is wearing a hood,' he said in his matter-of-fact Yorkshire way. 'He can't even hear you.'

I used to ride quite a bit for the top jumps trainer Jonjo O'Neill when he had Flat runners, and in the very early days I did consider whether to have a conversation with him about it. The thing is, jumping is something you've got to really want to do, and I didn't think I did: it was just a possible fall-back.

Without going as far as to say I was at a crossroads where I might have called it a day, I was more at a point where I needed to get out of a rut and almost reinvent what I was doing. So I got in touch with Guy Jewell, who lived locally in Marlborough and knew my father. He recalls a young George Baker, probably 14 but looking about eight, tapping him on the shoulder at Bath races asking him if he would put his £2 bets on for him. Guy was once an aspiring jump jockey with David Nicholson, and is now a successful Flat agent who played a major part in Hayley Turner's success.

I think Guy was pleased that I'd got in touch, and asked if we could meet up in the Bell at West Overton. Apparently he used to see Dermid Hyde in the pub, and when I was just getting started as an apprentice, Dermid had told him that he should take me on as

I would ride anything. But it had been November, towards the end of the Turf season, Guy was knackered from managing his stable of jockeys all the time, and I think the last thing he wanted then was to work flat out through the winter for some poxy teenager, so he said he couldn't sign me up. Pretty soon I had been absolutely flying, and now he was kicking himself.

Guy asked me what I wanted out of racing, and I told him I wanted more big winners, not only to raise my profile but also to start making a better living for myself. He replied that we had to work out what we could do to improve. Immediately he identified the problem: I had to put my minimum weight up. All I had been concentrating on was doing light weights, so I would get more rides which, as I reasoned, would produce more winners.

Guy, though, argued that I should concentrate on quality rather than quantity, getting rides on better horses with more of a chance of winning. I was obsessed with trying to make 8st 9lb to get rides, but it was making me weak and uncomfortable. If I wasn't feeling happy within myself, said Guy, I was never going to ride well, and it would help if I could eat a bit more. He said the best thing to do was to ride at a minimum of 8st 12lb, which we later moved to 9st.

Joining Guy was about the most sensible decision I made in my professional life. He managed me brilliantly. I'd become so greedy and driven that if it had been down to me, I'd have been riding my lightest weight every day, but he'd pick and choose, ensuring I was only doing my absolute minimum weight now and then for a really good ride, rather than for a small maiden race or something with no chance.

I'm sure there were plenty of rides on the table that I would have wanted to waste for that he never told me about in order to preserve my health. You will always have the numbers guys in the weighing room, who are just happy to get on as many horses as possible, but we decided that it would be more helpful to have ten fewer rides a week if it meant getting on a few better ones.

I'd trust Guy's judgement implicitly. If I rang him up and asked him if a horse was worth doing light on, I wouldn't question it if he said yes, and just get on with it. Thanks to Guy, I had a pretty good strike-rate on horses that I would ride at around my minimum weight. The introduction of 48-hour declarations in 2006 was a huge help to us, as much as almost everyone else in the sport moaned about it. It meant another day to organise our plans, not only from declaration stage but also with the six-day advance entries.

I started to feel better, look better, ride better and the winners came along. We got 40 winners that year, then reached our goal of 70 the following season. Later we made the target 100, and having achieved that, could start chasing the elite big-race winners. It's a bit like in football: if you're not scoring goals in the Championship, a Premier League team won't look twice at you. Those occasional chances you might get on a better horse are a bit like your moment in the transfer window: when people see you doing well on better-class horses, it's much easier to sell you to other owners for their horses. Riding for the likes of Chris Wall and Gary Moore helped me to turn the corner, but the key thing was to get some momentum in the first place. Guy says when I knocked on his door it was a bit like dropping a folder of paper on his office floor: everything was there to make it work – it just needed picking up, tidying and organising. And that's something he's extremely good at.

It can be a strange relationship between agent and jockey, as you work so closely and rely on each other – we would speak five or six times a day. Guy always said from his perspective as an agent that usually you're friends with your jockey client until you're sacked, and then you might as well delete their number from your phone as you won't hear from them again. That may well be true in general, but not with the two of us.

What I loved about him was that he'd always tell the truth, and never fill me with bollocks. From my position I just wanted someone to keep all of my trainers and owners happy. It was my job to ride and, if I fulfilled that side of the bargain, then other owners and trainers would notice me. My ability advertised me. It was Guy's responsibility to organise those commitments, and to make sure people didn't fall out.

Soon Guy and I had become very close mates, and might have gone on together until we both retired. He was the obvious choice to be the best man at my wedding, and even now I still call him three or four times a week. I expect he enjoyed the rest when I had my accident!

CHAPTER FOUR
THE HUNGERFORD SET

Looking back it was madness. Racing is an all-consuming job, you work hard every day, travelling around the country surviving on very little to eat, but if you have some success you can start making a few quid and as a young man in your early 20s, you're bound to want to let off some steam now and again. My method of relaxing and taking my mind off work came in the form of the age-old sport of drinking alcohol.

I wouldn't say I was ever a huge drinker or party animal, but I just loved the craic of a night out with the boys. I had put almost all of my savings into buying my own flat in Hungerford, and it offered a new-found freedom, especially with Sam Hitchcott, who sat next to me in the weighing room, living just down the road. A fellow resident in my block was the trainer Mick Channon's son Michael, generally known as Junior, who was downstairs. We were very much the three amigos, but there were a big bunch of other local jockeys around, such as Sam's brother Ben, Steve Drowne, Fergus Sweeney, Dane O'Neill and Liam Keniry.

Saturday was always our proper 'Give it a kick in the belly' night. We knew Jeremy Scott, the landlord of the Railway Tavern in Hungerford, and almost every evening began and finished there. Usually after waking up late on a Sunday morning I would end up ringing Jeremy to find out whether I had been well behaved. The problem was that I would never remember a night out, even if I thought I wasn't drinking that much.

It's drinking the shorts, the rum and cokes and the gin and tonics, that gets you. You feel fine in the pub, but then haven't a clue how you got home, and you wake up in bed with all your clothes on. On a couple of occasions I didn't make it through my front door, and just slept on the communal landing of the flats. Junior, who used to be involved in television and now very sensibly works with his dad, could have his moments too. He would always go home earlier than me, but when I got back his front door was always open, everything was on, even the cooker, and he was passed out somewhere. He was even an occasional sleepwalker, which made for some entertainment. It was really just the sort of stuff most 20-somethings do. I'd never get rowdy – perhaps someone might get a bit annoyed with you knocking drinks over or falling all over the place, but I'm not sure anyone would say I was a bad drunk.

Nevertheless, it was a strange way of behaving for a sports person: you would behave like a monk during the week, and then really the worst thing you could do at the weekend was to go out and drink a load. My weight would balloon, but with little racing on a Sunday you had plenty of time to get it back down in time for the regular Windsor summer evening meetings on the Monday. I wouldn't change any of those times – we were living the life – but I suppose it led to me being more focused on getting my weight right for the week than very driven for success.

Early in the winter of 2007 it all came to a head. It was a quiet period of the year, and I'd been out with the lads for a couple of nights in a row, but a few of them wanted to go out yet again on the Saturday. I was down to ride at Kempton on the Sunday, so I said to myself that I would just go for some dinner, make my excuses and slip off for an early night. No sooner were we in Casanovas in Hungerford and I had a glass of wine in my hand, than the evening developed into something like that film *The Hangover*.

I woke up in bed at about 10 a.m. not remembering anything. I found out that I'd been displaying some of my brutal dancing skills in a club in Newbury and hadn't got in until 4 a.m. Unsurprisingly, having visited the kebab house as well as consuming a load of alcohol,

I was heavy as lead at 9st 7lb, which was a lot for me at any point during my career. There was an hour and a half before I had to leave for Kempton, and I had to lose three or four pounds if I was going to make the weight for my first ride.

I jumped straight in the bath and sat in there for half an hour, and normally I'd drop two pounds just like that. I had a bottle of water while I was in there, but when I got out, I'd literally not lost anything because I was that dry from a night out. So I got back in for another 20 minutes and managed to lose half a pound.

Panic was beginning to set in. There was only one thing for it, I knew; I was going to have to sweat in the car. I put my silver sweat suit on, sweated all the way down to Kempton and, despite feeling absolutely horrific, it sort of seemed as if everything was going to be all right. Unfortunately, I didn't sweat at all well, and just felt sick. Convinced as I was that I must definitely have lost two pounds during the drive, I dived on the scales at the course and discovered I'd only lost half a pound. I still had two and a half pounds to get off in the sauna. I thought, 'Shit. It's not going to happen.'

I'll never forget the response of Brian Yorke, my valet. He'd seen what weight I was carrying, and could obviously smell that my breath still stank of drink – I'm sure if the testers had been there that day I wouldn't have passed a breathalyser. 'I'll give you one piece of advice,' he said: 'You look awful. The best you can do is to get the hell out of here before anyone sees you.'

And that's what I did. I bolted before the officials had arrived, leaving with the excuse that I just felt unwell. I'm not a fellow who cries very often, but I got back in the car and just broke down. It wasn't a mental breakdown or anything – I just kept thinking, 'What a fucking idiot I am.' I had let down John Best, the trainer I was due to ride for that day, in particular, not to mention myself.

There had been a couple of similar episodes in the past which had been warning signs, and I'd behaved myself for maybe a week or so and then relapsed. This had been building. I put on quite a good front with most people around me, but someone I confided in is Junior. I rang him up and cried like a pussy. He was buzzing from having a winner that day so in his usually reassuring way, said 'Don't worry mate. Pull your self together. Man-up and move on.'

As I drove home, a bit more composed, I realised I had to sort myself out. The other person I needed to tell the whole truth to was Guy Jewell. I rang him later and explained what happened. He gave me similar tough love and told me that I was a bloody idiot and that either I had to learn to conduct myself better or pack up.

On the way home I stopped at Halfords and bought a pushbike, and when I got back to Hungerford I cycled all the way to Lambourn, saw another mate Frankie McDonald, who used to ride and ended up being a sort of informal driver for me for a few years, and cycled back home. Funnily enough, I don't think I ever used that bike a second time – it's probably still locked up in the apartment block in Hungerford. Nonetheless, my attitude was beginning to change. You hit points that make you knuckle down, and at that time I had my head up my arse and wasn't aware of what I was doing.

I didn't suddenly become an angel, by any means. I just started to do things in a more sensible way. When I had some spare time I'd continue to go out and have fun and a drink and dinner on weekends. I'd just try not to do it all the time. It was probably a slightly different, more sociable era in the weighing room back then: it wasn't frowned upon for lads to go out quite a lot. Back then a lot of us were probably playing at the job. It was Tony McCoy's single-minded and meticulous professionalism which completely changed jockeys' mindsets.

As you get a bit older, you do naturally settle down, but Guy says it was getting together with Nicola that really changed me. Predictably enough, I met her in the Tavern on New Year's Eve in 2008. It's probably a good job it hadn't been the previous year in the exact same place when it was fancy dress and I had been dressed as a blonde prostitute. Luckily this year, I was in my usual jockey uniform of fake Guccis and Levi jeans.

I sort of knew of Nicola, who is five years younger than me, as she worked for Hughie Morrison's stable half an hour away in East Ilsley. Her sister was in my year at Park House and she had grown up in Newbury. We had found ourselves in the sport through very different routes. Nicola had studied at Hartpury College, a specialist equine university in Gloucestershire, and been to work for Mary Gordon-Watson (now Low), who won a team gold medal at the 1972 Munich Olympics at eventing before turning her hand to breaking in and pre-training horses in our area for the likes of the Queen and Roger Charlton. Nicola had decided to move into racing, and had lined up interviews with Hughie, Roger and Andrew Balding. She was offered a job by Hughie on the spot and didn't even go to the other two interviews. In terms of our paths crossing at just the right time, I'm very glad she didn't.

To be honest, I haven't a clue what I said to Nicola that night in the pub, but she made a big impression on me. Like all single lads would, I did a bit of Facebook stalking, and she accepted my friend request.

Just after New Year, I went off on a skiing holiday with a load of the lads and assorted waifs and strays, which was something of a tradition. You will get the gist of those holidays if I explain what had happened one year when we were delayed flying out of Gatwick for about four hours. Seven or eight of us decided to play a few rounds of

Spoof, a guessing game involving the amount of coins you are hiding inside your hand. The losers would have to buy bottles of champagne. Whoever lost the last round before we got on the plane, the deal was that they would have to do the last run of the day on the slopes in their pants or shorts. I was the one who got stung, and there was no chance of getting out of it. I got down to the bottom in my shorts, while a few of them were darting in and out trying to put me on my arse.

At the end of the holiday we decided this time to get some of those short skis and were just messing about on them. I was about to do a little jump when I had a bit of a wobble and the most pathetic fall you've ever seen. I headbutted the ground and bust my nose, which is large enough anyway. There was blood everywhere, absolutely gushing out red patches on the white snow. I just stuffed it up with cotton wool and carried on, as I had broken it before getting headbutted by horses. Junior had filmed the incident and now stuck it up on Facebook, so at least people wouldn't assume I'd got a slap off someone.

It also made for a good icebreaker after I got back when I decided to send a message to Nicola. She agreed to go out with me to a Chinese restaurant, and although I don't think I impressed her with my sophistication by eating chicken chow mein with a spoon, I must have done well enough to get a second date. Things developed, and I always joke that Nicola managed to worm her way in pretty quickly, but my settling down and being more mature was not such an immediate thing.

A lot of the time Sam, I and a few of the others would still have a few on a Saturday night and go out clubbing, and if I had a Sunday free, Nicola and I would go out for Sunday lunch for what would turn into a bit of a session. I might not be too busy on the Monday, but she would still have to get up first thing and go off to Hughie's for work, and when she got back late in the morning I would often still be in bed nursing my hangover.

I still could be a bit of loose cannon at times, and couldn't just go out for a few beers: if I was out, I was out. It came to a head one night when we were in the Tavern. I wanted to go clubbing – I think Nicola was working the next day or didn't fancy it. So I did, sneaking out of the back door, turning my phone off and leaving her there in the pub on her own. It wasn't very chivalrous behaviour, and it became plain that if I carried on like I was doing at the weekends when I wasn't riding, she was going to leave me.

Sam and I have often talked about the positive influences our wives have had on us. He met Harriet a little while before I met Nicola, at a time when he was struggling a bit with his career. Having more focus meant he ended up getting a very good job as second jockey for the top Dubai trainer Doug Watson. I, meanwhile, got control of my weight and gave my career considerable longevity.

My rather irresponsible behaviour three or four years after Nicola and I met has meant that unfortunately she won't come on another of our skiing trips. A big group of us had taken a chalet in Val d'Isère, including Sam and Harriet, Hayley Turner, J-P Guillambert, Kelly Harrison (now Guillambert) and J-P's sister Francoise. I seem to remember Chris Catlin and James Doyle having to share the last room as neither had girlfriends at the time.

Nicola had been skiing once before when she was about 13, and she was doing pretty well, following us along and managing to get down one black run unscathed. Unfortunately, I led us down a path towards La Face, a very famous piste which was used as part of the course for the downhill at the 1992 Winter Olympics. It's extremely steep and there was no alternative route. Nicola didn't take this very well and just couldn't do it, which was all the more humiliating for her because we all had walkie-talkies and the others could hear her crying, and me reasoning with her and telling her to take off her skis and slide down on her bum. Understandably after that she didn't fancy going out with us, and for the rest of the week pottered around on the easy greens.

Nicola was held in very high regard at Hughie's yard, where she was pupil assistant trainer for a time as well as an office secretary, and she really knows her stuff on the medical and organisational side of things. She also rode him three winners as an amateur rider, and managed to get a ride in the big lady riders' race at Ascot on King George day on Sohraab, whom we had at home for a while after he retired. Because she was quite light, Hughie was pushing her to become an apprentice, but her heart wasn't in it to be a full-time jockey: it was just something she enjoyed doing for a spell. Nicola continued to work for Hughie until she took maternity leave in 2016 when she was expecting our daughter Isabella.

She was a brilliant rider at home, riding quite a few of Hughie's nicer horses, but I don't think I helped when she was on the racecourse. She rode a really good race tactically, but when she was pushing a horse along she couldn't get down low enough. I wasn't very complimentary about how she looked, which I think knocked her confidence, and eventually I suspect she had simply had enough of me being harsh and taking the piss. Riding came so naturally to me, and with hindsight I ought to have been more encouraging by offering her lessons and helping her out.

It was also a shame that I wasn't there for her first-ever ride at Southwell, a very difficult place to be starting out. It's such hard work riding for a mile and three-quarters on the Fibresand surface.

She just got knackered, but afterwards the stewards decided to pull her in, and gave her a 10-day ban as a non-trier, which was a bizarre and shocking decision.

The first time you go into the stewards' room is like being thrown to the lions: you haven't got a clue what's happening, and you don't know what to say to them. Junior jockeys are allowed to go into the room with someone, and I wish I had been there to help her out. Nicola didn't carry on in the saddle for that long, just a year and a half, but anyone who rides winners can claim it as a big achievement – you can't take that away from them.

By this time I was starting to do better, and had enough money to be able to upgrade from my flat. After Nicola had moved in with me in Hungerford and given up her room in East Ilsley, the amount of driving was starting to affect her. To get to Hughie's in the morning and back a few hours later for evening stables meant that she was spending at least a couple of hours in the car every day.

One Sunday we spotted a new development of houses at Chilton just off the A34. We walked into the show home and struck a deal there and then. Our house was two minutes from Hughie's, and the location was better for me too, as there wasn't quite the immediate temptation of an evening in the pubs of Hungerford. The Tavern was sold around that time, and quite a few of our friends were getting married, having children and moving out of town, so perhaps things were drawing to a natural conclusion anyway.

Nicola and I got married in Barbados in 2015. It was particularly special that my parents, who virtually never go away because my dad is always working, were able to come out. I knew they would be apprehensive about it, but two days before we left we found out they had already booked to go out again the following year.

I think Guy was under the impression that he was only going to be involved as an usher – he says I thrust the best man duties on him – but he was the only person I was ever going to choose. It meant he had to come up with a speech without much notice, but he's the sort of person who is good at things like that, and he nailed it. As he finished his speech, he gave me a clear plastic bag filled with Viagra-like blue smarties. My Mum piped up, 'perhaps I could use those on your Dad!'

I think a lot of my problems before I settled down were down to not having enough other interests – my getaway had always been going for dinner and a few beers – but by this time I was also getting into the far more grown-up sport of golf.

The jump jockey Dominic Elsworth got me into the sport by taking me to the West Berkshire club a few times. Just being out there for four hours with the phone off was really therapeutic, and far better for me than drinking. You've got to keep your wits about you in a game of golf, and it played to my competitive nature. For the first couple of years I got quite intense about it, and would keep turning up with new clubs and the latest bits of kit in the hope that it would bring about a change in my fortunes.

Having a bit of height helped me to drive the ball pretty far when I got a good connection, but putting was more of a problem. It frustrated me so much that I bought a little putting machine and practised relentlessly in the flat through the winter. It used to amuse Dom that I would get onto the green, but it would usually take at least three shots to get down from there. Then suddenly, when I turned up on the course the next season, my putter was like a wand, and I was sinking balls from everywhere. I got down to having a handicap of about 14 for the first couple of years – this might have changed a little on occasion – and would often join a few of the other jockeys on short golfing breaks around Europe when there were quiet spells in

One of my early riding experiences with Dad

A budding farrier, two years old and helping Dad in 1983

Dad gives me the leg-up on to my first, but sadly not last, camel in Jerusalem

Looking the part, almost, while riding work. I caught the bug early

Fresh faced and unaware of how little I would be able to eat for the rest of my career

Tedworth Hunt Pony Club Trials in August 1996. Riding Copper was always a buzz

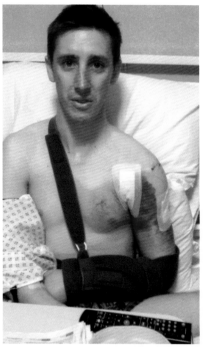

On a ski holiday in January 2009, having lost a game of Spoof at the airport before boarding the plane, this was my forfeit

The joys of life as a jockey, one of my far too frequent visits to hospital after a fall at Wolverhampton

Hands off! Nicola's mine

The Hungerford Set at Sam Hitchcott's wedding. As ever, Mick Channon jnr (second from right) knew how to accessorise

Nicola and I recharging the batteries in Cuba. The sharks there are particularly friendly

Seal Of Approval became my first Group 1 winner in the Qipco British Champions Fillies & Mares Stakes at Ascot on Champions Day 2013

Another Group 1 filly, Nicola Dumelow, said yes and we married in Barbados, 2015

My agent and best man, Guy Jewell and I decide it is worth learning to paddle board

Interception won the 2015 Wokingham Stakes for me at Royal Ascot

Racing Post *Editor Bruce Millington (second left) presented the prizes to my old boss, Bjorn Nielsen (centre), me and Interception's trainer, David Lanigan (right)*

I just managed to get beat on one of the best horses I ever rode, Al Kazeem (farside), in the 2014 Qipco Champion Stakes at Ascot

I took my time at Goodwood in 2009 but the legend that is Premio Loco put his head in front on the line. We won 11 races together

Nicola looks after Premio Loco in retirement, here they are in the dressage arena

the season or we had picked up suspensions. It was a bit different to the sort of holidays I used to have, such as the time when I went with jockeys Chris Catlin and Jamie Mackay to the notorious Mexican party resort of Cancun as teenagers, and someone asked us where our parents were.

Although my behaviour had improved, I could get away with the odd mad session, and one of the most fun times I ever had was going over to Clonmel for the National Coursing Finals, held on Clonmel racecourse. Liam Keniry, who is always known as 'Budgie', loved greyhounds and was always going on about this particular event, which is an Irish institution and the equivalent of the Waterloo Cup, the showpiece event in Britain before hare coursing was banned.

Liam had a dog which had qualified for the knockout tournament. This is apparently really tough, and I think he had been offered a few quid for it by other owners, but everyone told him to keep the dog because you could spend your life finding another one good enough to take part. It sounded as if it could be a laugh, so Liam, Sam, Jamie Spencer and I rode at Kempton on the Saturday, got a flight over and went to stay with Liam's parents. A guy we all knew called Victor, a good friend of the former jockey Barry Fenton, ran a pub near where they lived and we got on the pool table. As Jamie, Sam and I weren't bad pool players, we managed to hustle the locals for a few quid. Word seemed to get out about these outsiders, and more and more people turned up to take us on, but we kept our heads above water. This was after the indoor smoking ban had been introduced, but it hadn't stopped the 40 or 50 people crammed into this little room from puffing away. Although I would have been more than a little the worse for wear anyway, the fag smoke was so thick I could barely see the table.

By about half one in the morning, the Garda had turned up. Strangely, they weren't at all bothered about the smoking, but I think they wanted to break up the party. Victor told the officer we were staying in the pub so were allowed to be in there, and in the end they just asked us to turn the music down a bit and the party continued. It was a session and a half, as the Irish just don't go to bed. Liam's parents were out with us, his mum was up making sandwiches that night, and after only a couple of hours' kip she was back in the kitchen preparing us a fry-up to keep us going for our day out at Clonmel.

Liam's dog was odds-on to win his first course. The rules, which the others all knew far more about, are simple enough. Someone slips the hare loose and shortly afterwards a pair of dogs, which are muzzled, go after it, and the first one to get to the hare and turn its direction wins. We thought 'Happy days', lumped a few euros on Liam's dog in the belief that it would be paying for our trip, and decided that if it got through, we would stay the extra day. This idea didn't last long, as Liam's dog ran like its legs had been tied together.

It's a crazy event, and attracts all corners of society. There were a fair few racing faces around including the trainer Sir Mark Prescott, who is a huge coursing enthusiast. But the strangest thing of all was that hanging around with Jamie Spencer was like being in the presence of a rock star. He's from Tipperary, and I suppose you forget sometimes that he had been a hugely successful champion jockey in Ireland. Earlier I had wondered what was going on when he bought a pen from the service station on the way to Clonmel; later it became clear it was for all the autographs he needed to sign.

The main thing the punters wanted was a tip, and they were all coming up asking him if he fancied anything. All he would say to them was that Mark Johnston's horse would win at Wolverhampton that afternoon. I'm not sure he had even looked at the paper, or really had any sort of knowledge about the race; it was just a short-priced favourite in a maiden or something.

There was a little Tote building at Clonmel, and everyone piled in there to watch this race on the television. I'm not joking when I say it felt as if the roof nearly came off the stands when the horse just got up on the line under Joe Fanning. The place just erupted, even if they had probably only had five euros on it. It's a good job Jamie hadn't told everyone there a different horse.

Afterwards we went off to a Chinese restaurant in Clonmel called Ming's, where everyone also seemed to know Jamie, from the guy who owned it to the local priest. It had been a fair session, and I have a hazy memory of Sam being put in a baby chair whilst we were eating. Jamie also bought some champagne and invited a few of the people in the restaurant over to our table for a glass before shaking the bottle up like a Formula One driver and absolutely soaking everyone. It was the sort of idea that might see you getting a slap in England, but as they sort of knew Jamie, it was all taken in very good spirits.

It was one of those times you never forget, but it probably took me a week to get over it, having had about three hours' sleep in three days. I was a broken man when I came back to Nicola.

CHAPTER FIVE
GETTING IN A SWEAT

Weight is the obsession that every jockey wished he didn't have and only winning or the thought of winning can make it bearable. I would know to the pound, if not almost to the ounce, what I weighed at almost every hour around the clock. What the scales said when I first stood on them in the morning would almost always have to be less by the time I raced in the afternoon. I was an athlete but dehydration was part of my preparation.

It is only since I retired and started talking to Nicola about my lifestyle that I realised how much of my time, both mentally and physically, had been spent dealing with my weight. Particularly in my later years, it was how I planned out my entire day. Now that Guy had put my weight up I was no longer quite on the absolute limit of the lightest possible weight I could physically do, but being so tall still meant that even my amended minimum weight would require constant management. When I'd speak to Guy about my future rides, it was never about which horse I was riding or what chance it had, it was about where I was going and what weight I had to do. Then I would know whether I would be able to go out for dinner and see how I would have to structure my time.

I suppose I didn't have a lot else to worry about in my life apart from knowing how many pounds I would have to lose, and the first thing I would do after waking every morning was to get on the scales. I reckon I got to know my body so well that I would be able to guess almost exactly what the reading would be. It would rarely be a pleasant surprise; I think that I could probably count on one hand the times I was amazed at how light I was. It's quite depressing really, but it's just the way it was, and I don't think I ever had time to think about what it would be like otherwise, or to be jealous of the smaller and lighter jockeys who could eat what they fancied.

When I was younger, there were some more unpleasant surprises, when I couldn't figure out why I was suddenly 9st 5lb when I had done 9st 1lb the day before. The truth is that it was a battle I was never going to win, and at times it was very demoralising, but thankfully I got into a good place with it as I adopted a more sensible routine.

Initially, though, I was approaching the process incorrectly, and my weight would yo-yo. I would use the racecourse sauna to sweat off the final few pounds before a race, but I managed it in the wrong way. There used to be a notion that if you just sat in there for an hour you would lose the weight, but what was never mentioned is that after you rode, you would have a couple of bottles of water to feel a bit better, and it just sits there. Your body holds on to it, and you become like a sponge.

If I was doing light the next day, I would never eat anything the night before, because in my mind that was the right thing to do. As I learned more about controlling my weight, I realised that you have got to fuel the fire. If you want to work hard and work the weight off, then not eating or drinking is not the right answer. After all, you wouldn't really go to the gym for an hour and a half and expect to have a good workout if you started off dehydrated.

Times have changed since I began as an apprentice, and more people have worked on programmes for jockeys. Dr George Wilson at Liverpool John Moores University, in particular, has studied the weight loss programmes used by jockeys and produced diet and exercise programmes. The experts all say you've got to kick-start your metabolism in the mornings, and that the sauna should be more of a last resort. What I found out is that I operated far better when I lost the weight more gradually, and towards the end, because my weight was more consistent, I would very rarely have to use the sauna at the races. It would continually frustrate me seeing the younger lads going into the sauna to lose a pound, knowing that if they had been on the ball and more organised, getting the weight off more steadily, they would feel a lot better. There was a diet programme, which has evolved a bit since my day, and it had some funky old suggestions featuring cottage cheese and eggs, but it did work when stuck to rigidly, provided I could have a cheat day on a Sunday.

I spoke to Dr Wilson quite a bit about the subject and did a fair bit of my own reading. He had a few strange suggestions, including sending you this stuff to drink, then once a day you have to pee in a test tube and put it in the freezer. It gets taken away, and from it they can read the energy expenditure, so you have a guide on how much you need to balance your input and output.

One of the lads I admired a lot, who changed the whole approach, was Johnny Murtagh, the brilliant Irish jockey who also had difficulties with his weight. When he first started coming to England to ride for a few trainers, you would always see him at the races running around the track with a sweatsuit on, and he'd only go to the sauna for the final couple of pounds. He made me realise there was another way of doing things.

When I reached the peak of my career I would not have to ride out for trainers as often – maybe only once or twice a week – because it was more important to be at my best for the races. I'd get up and have breakfast, which was poached eggs on one of those really small pieces of brown bread. I felt it got me going, and I would drink a fair amount of green tea and water in order to sweat better, so much so that Roger Charlton's wife Clare ended up buying me my own teapot to make it in when I was at their yard.

If I woke up and needed to lose two pounds, I'd know exactly how long that would take. Without absolutely knackering myself, I would take the dogs out and run up to the Ridgeway from my house, power walk along the top and walk back, which would take me between 35 and 50 minutes. I knew I would always lose between 1.5lb and 2lb doing that, depending upon how heavy I was, and if it was winter time I would put more clothes on to make me sweat more. Then I would come back, run the bath and sit in it, knowing I could lose another 2lb in an hour and 20 minutes without feeling shattered. Then the harder stuff would come. I had a Jacuzzi bath and a TV in the room, I had connected my phone up and I could read the paper. The bathroom basically became my office.

It isn't something everyone could do; Nicola remembers coming into a boiling hot bathroom to find me slumped on the floor with a towel over my head, eyes bloodshot. She would sometimes cut the end off an ice pop so I could have a little something to cool me down. It was hard, hard work, but it was the route I had chosen, and I did what I had to do to continue being a jockey.

I've never been a big lunch person, but if you're racing there's always something to choose from in the tea room. If there was something like a chicken curry, I'd fill a small polystyrene cup halfway and just pick at it. That would be enough to keep me going during the day, then after a few rides I might have a slice of chocolate or something.

I always found the nutrition side quite interesting. Obviously if you're having a meal, you must eat something proper, but if you're just picking, I think it can be anything provided it's something small. In my mind I could either have a quarter of a sandwich or a much larger portion of salad, but I'd rather have the sandwich as it's something I liked. It's all moderation.

I would always have dinner with Nicola, even if it was only some chicken breast or lean pork and salad or vegetables. I'd just have to make sure it wasn't too late, always before 8 p.m. because I didn't sleep very well if I had a full stomach – not that I ever really had that. Nicola was incredibly thoughtful about it. Once we were sat down she would only eat what I ate, and would have a bigger lunch when I was out rather than having a nice big spaghetti bolognese while I was stuck eating leaves. She also found some smaller crockery, which can trick the eyes into thinking you've eaten more.

Eating healthily was more of a challenge during my bachelor days living in Hungerford. I quite like fish, and it's good for you, but I always found it really hard to cook, and I started going to Waitrose and buying it with the sauce and all the instructions in a bag. I was going to go skint doing that all the time – it was costing more than going out for dinner! The Casanova Italian restaurant was also just at the back of my old flat, and at one stage I would get takeaway from there almost every night – not eating bad food or anything – but I must have almost kept them in business. They did know me pretty well by the end.

When I became a bit more successful in my final four or five years, it made another huge difference when I was able to hire Frankie McDonald as my driver.

I would never do as many miles as someone like Joe Fanning, who is based with Mark Johnston in Yorkshire but seems to appear in a different part of the country every day, but even doing 60 or 70,000 miles a year is an awful lot when you're driving on your own. Frankie being at the wheel meant that I could have a nap or do the form on the way to the track and could stop and have dinner on the way home. Nicola noticed that I was in far better form – less gaunt-looking, and less grumpy. A lot of the jockeys who live near each other still shared lifts, but my routine forced me to be a bit anti-social. I needed to set my own times for my routine – even someone being a bit late collecting me could risk messing up my weight – and I would be factoring in a bit of extra time in case the traffic was bad. My aim was always to get to the races half a pound under what I needed to be for my ride, as when you were operating on such fine margins, there could be occasional difficulties.

Not everyone will know that the racing colours of owners come in different varieties. There are thicker, heavier versions which weigh just under 1lb, and a lighter, slightly more expensive version which weighs 0.1 lb. The colours are kept by the trainer, and there would often have been both the light and heavy sets available, but which one they actually brought would be vital, especially if I was struggling on the limit. It mattered so much that I would pretty much know which of my regular owners had both sets, and it got to the point where I would ring certain trainers just to make sure they brought the light ones. It was one of my biggest pet hates when the lad or lass bringing the horse to the races put the wrong colours in the lorry.

You have to weigh out for a race with all your riding kit on, including your saddle, and you are technically given a 2lb allowance for your equipment, as you have to wear a body protector. The clerk of the scales, who oversees this procedure, does give you a tiny bit of leniency, but for me every ounce counted. I had sponsored breeches, which were not quite made of paper but were still incredibly light, and often I wouldn't even wear a top under the colours, just a small necktie, to save a little more.

The saddle was crucial too – whenever I was abroad I was always on the lookout for new gear. I suppose it's slightly bending the rules, but it's also just part of playing the game. I managed to find a really light saddle from an Australian company called Persuader, which was 0.2lb lighter than the one I had before. It sounds ridiculous, but that was a really big breakthrough. It was tiny, strengthened with carbon fibre rather than metal, and was essentially just some stirrup leathers and something you can put on the horse's girth so you can ride a horse. These saddles, which look very different from the recreational ones, would have a short shelf life, and I'd reckon to be able to get 400 rides out of one before it got weaker. They would cost a few hundred quid to replace, but it wasn't exactly something I could live without.

You are allowed to weigh in after the race 1lb heavier than you were to start with, so you can have a little drink of water, but there are quite serious penalties from the stewards if the difference is greater. There are silly things you can do to push the boundaries: racecourses have these all-singing, all-dancing scales, but at certain racecourses there will be a certain spot on the scales you can stand on and know you will be 0.1lb lighter. I'd spend so much time at Lingfield during the winters and when a new set of scales arrived there, I discovered that if you stood just on the left-hand side of the yellow box on them, you'd be just a tiny bit lighter than you would be in the middle.

Don't get me wrong. I'd pull the odd stunt when it was really difficult to make the weight. Back in the day I would sometimes try to take the girth off and just have the surcingle wrapped around my saddle to distract the clerk. I would know that most stables would have a spare girth in their bag and that could be 1lb saved. I remember one time, when I was really struggling, a trainer suggested I even handed my saddle out of the back door of the weighing room to him and to weigh out without it!

Nowadays, the clerks of the scales are so switched on that you'd have to be fairly clever to get away with anything devious, but I'm sure the jockeys of the past had some quite crafty tricks up their sleeves.

On occasion – I wouldn't say I had to do it all the time – I've had to lose half a stone in a day. You don't feel great afterwards, I can tell you. When I was younger I'm sure it affected the standard of my riding, as I was only bothered about doing stupidly light weights and didn't even care how the horses ran. It's like when you first start drinking: you're not as good at hiding that you were drunk the night before. When you've had a big night out and you have to go back into the office for a day's work, it's always a lot harder and slower to do everything.

Without you realising it, dehydration is going to affect your reaction times, as you simply can't be as sharp when you've been sweating all day. Worse still, sometimes I used to get cramp in my hands. It wouldn't happen when I was in action at the races, luckily, but when I was driving home my hands would sometimes lock up like claws, simply through dehydration. Back in the day, it was said, many more jockeys would use diuretics, or 'piss pills', to keep the weight down, but when I first came into racing I didn't even know what they were, and didn't come across anyone who used them. Ian Mongan once got caught for taking them back in 2001, and it's not something you can hide as they stay in your system and the officials can trace them. If people are still using them, they certainly don't talk about it.

Jockeys control their weights in loads of different ways, but the most controversial method is by 'flipping', or making yourself sick. It's a taboo subject and something the racing authorities have been working hard to stop, but whether people like to believe it or not, it still happens. I only tried it once. When I was in Newmarket to ride out I often stayed overnight with J-P Guillambert, a close friend who has gone on to have a good career out in Qatar. He used to flip as a way of maintaining his weight. We were at his house, talking about what we would do for dinner, and he said he was having a Domino's Pizza. I knew I couldn't eat much, as I was quite heavy, but I thought I'd be able to have one slice, or perhaps a small one. He said, 'Just have a large one and flip it.'

So I ate a whole Domino's Pizza, and then had to make myself sick by sticking my fingers down my throat. Only it didn't work. I stood over the toilet bowl for 15 or 20 minutes, heaving, but with nothing coming out.

I'll never forget looking into the mirror after I'd given up: I saw I'd broken the blood vessels in my eyes because I had been trying so hard. The reason, I realised, was because I'd been eating the wrong food. People who do that sort of thing know that if you eat pizza and want to flip it, you'd have to be a real pro, because it's so stodgy and sits in your stomach. I wasn't, so if I'd had pasta instead, or something that came in small bits, that would have been much easier to bring back up.

It was probably a blessing in disguise, because it's such an easy way of losing weight, and if it had worked I might have been tempted to carry on. Instead, I felt like a prat and was still as heavy as lead. It was one of those lightbulb moments. If I'd had to flip to sort my weight out, I'd soon have given up. It also felt to me almost like cheating.

Top jockeys such as Kieren Fallon have spoken about how flipping goes on, and I think a lot of the younger lads copied those who did it. I can't speak for how it is now, but for a lot of young lads it is honestly just mind over matter. You have a big feed, make yourself sick, and you don't feel hungry because mentally you have eaten and feel full. The other problem is that if you start flipping and then stop, your weight balloons. It also can't be healthy just eating rubbish and not leaving anything in your body, or only picking at something small rather than digesting a healthy meal. They would probably say sweating is just as bad.

It's a personal choice whether you decide to flip, and most people are old enough to know what they're doing and make their own decisions. Only once did I ever say anything about it to anybody, on a day when I had got to York very early to walk the track. I was in the toilet, and in the cubicle next to me I could hear someone trying to be sick. As I was washing my hands I asked the young lad what he'd been trying to do – had he actually eaten anything?

'No.'

'So how are you going to make yourself sick if there's nothing in your stomach?' He must have seen other people doing it, but not really understood why or how it worked.

Occasionally there were moments of black humour. There used to be a tea boy at Sandown called Slav, a big, friendly guy who would sort out the food for the jockeys and always help you out if you wanted something to take home with you. Many years ago, he had set out a big vat of curry and rice on the hotplate and one jockey had sat down and eaten a massive plate of it. Then he had gone to the toilet to go and flip. Slav had followed him in, presumably to go for a pee, and heard the sound of vomiting. He came literally sprinting into the tea room shouting, 'Put the curry down, such-and-such is being sick!' in case we were all going to get food poisoning!

I'm told flipping is a big part of the culture in America, where they actually have special bins in the weighing room, and I find that quite sad. But is it any sadder than getting in the bath and taking 4lb off? I don't know. I've often thought that if I had flipped I could have been quite a bit lighter and maybe have had a better career. But you just don't know.

After I retired, someone at the gym asked me what food I'd missed not being able to eat when I was a jockey. It was strange, because I'd been controlling my weight for so long I rarely thought about anything I particularly missed. But I did love pizza, and that's about the worst thing you can eat. If I had a day off, I always had a soft spot for Pizza Express pizzas – they're quite light and not that doughy. Even at my heaviest, I'd manage to cram one of those in at least once a month. I suppose it would have been possible to have pizza every night, but certainly only a slice for that little hit, rather than a whole one. Eating more was just a luxury that I couldn't afford.

Strangely, the only thing that works differently is alcohol. If you went out and had a couple of beers, you'd be very heavy from it. But if you went out for ten, sometimes you'd be lighter the next day as you'd have peed it all out. As I found, though, it would catch you up a couple of days later, as obviously you'd been dehydrated. But beers became a better solution for when I was having a drink than the spirits which had got me in such trouble in the early days.

As organised as I became, there would occasionally be a spanner in the works. I once accepted the offer to go to Singapore to ride Secret Asset, a horse I had finished an agonising second aboard in the previous year's Prix de l'Abbaye, in the 2012 Krisflyer International Sprint. His trainer Jane Chapple-Hyam had planned it all out, and I rode in England on the Friday, flew on Saturday and arrived with the time difference on the Sunday morning. I had about five hours until the race and had planned my brief visit carefully, knowing I would have to make a weight of 57kg, or just under 9st. I even had the luxury of having a little bit of food and a drink on the plane, and with the help of a sleeping pill I managed to get nine and a half hours' rest. I actually felt great from such a long flight, and when I arrived in Singapore I was surprisingly light at 9st 2lb, so I only had a little bit to lose and plenty of time in which to do it in the racecourse sauna.

Unfortunately, when I walked into the weighing room at the state-of-the-art Kranji racecourse, there was no sauna. Well, there was, but it was chained up because they had banned it being used. All sorts of things started going through my head, but the main one was 'How the fuck am I going to do the weight?'

As it was so warm over there, I came up with a new plan. I asked Alan Munro, the Derby-winning jockey who had become one of the top figures in Singapore, whether he had any waterproof gear. He did, but there is quite a size difference between Alan and me: when I put his breeches and top on they were absolutely skin-tight. I also borrowed a pair of trainers from another jockey that were too small for me, and went for a run. Only I couldn't use the track, because they had closed it for the racing, so I had to settle for running around the car park instead.

I must have looked quite comical, but I didn't feel it. It was so humid I thought I was going to die. When I got back on the scales I had lost some of the weight, but there was still a bit to go. I couldn't do another run; I was already rock bottom, and I think I would have passed out.

Thankfully there was a British guy I knew who was training over there called James Peters and the racecourse organised a car to take me to his apartment block where there was a sauna. I got the weight off, rushed back and Secret Asset ran a blinder to finish third.

I've never, ever felt so dehydrated, and it was a lesson learned. When I was fortunate enough to be asked by Jane to ride Mull Of Killough in another Group 1 at the same international meeting a year later, I got there three days early and settled in.

Most of my trainers did not have international-type horses, so I did not get to ride in Australia or America, but I thought that Singapore was an amazing place once I had the time to see more than a taxi and the racecourse car park. There is a fantastic atmosphere at Kranji, with everything based around the one track, and I did look into whether you could apply to ride as an international jockey over the winter. Story of my life: under Singapore rules I was too heavy to be given a licence, and I was stuck spending the colder months driving to Lingfield and Wolverhampton once again.

Occasionally they talk about phasing the saunas out of British racecourses too, but I think it would only mean jockeys finding different ways to lose weight. What's to stop someone going to a leisure centre or a hotel to find a sauna or steam room, or sweating in the car with loads of clothes on and the heaters on full blast (which I did quite a lot when I was younger)? It may not make athletic sense but dehydration is the only way we have found to do it.

CHAPTER SIX
MY STRONGEST SUPPORTERS

What a young jockey needs is not so much the headlines but safe hands around when he hits them. I lost my claim at Leicester on 27 May 2002, and while I had never threatened to win the champion apprentice title nor ridden for particularly high profile stables, I was starting to develop what were to be my two longest-standing partnerships – with Chris Wall and Gary Moore. You won't find two safer pairs of hands in the sport.

It was Richard Mullen, a regular rider for Chris, who gave me the push in the right direction and put in a good word that I was a nice young lad. Chris had noticed that I was doing reasonably well and seemed to like the way that I rode, so he agreed to give me a chance when one came along. Towards the end of the 2000 season I was still claiming 5lb when Chris put me up on a little horse of his at Newbury called Bonaguil, and he seemed satisfied when it won.

We let things develop and other opportunities began to come along to take me to the next level. Aside from one occasion when I think I nearly gave Chris a heart attack, by misjudging where I was supposed to pull up a horse on one of Newmarket's less familiar gallops and almost careered into a band of trees, we had the perfect relationship right up to the end of my career.

I don't know exactly what defines a good trainer, but with the horses he has Chris is just a genius. That word is shouted out a lot, but he's genuinely so, so clever and on the ball. Although he did not have a massive string of horses when I joined up with him, and still doesn't, he's always been a very well-respected figure in the racing community in Newmarket. He tends to keep his jockeys in-house and always made me feel very welcome.

Chris worked for some of the best in the game – Barry Hills, Luca Cumani and Sir Mark Prescott – and obviously some of that education, particularly in being careful with horses, has rubbed off on him. His biggest trademark is that he's very patient: he gives horses more time if they need it, and doesn't rush them to the racecourse if he thinks they are still immature. Maiden races can be very competitive, full of well-bred horses from the big stables, and he would know very soon if one of his two-year-olds would be good enough to win one. If they weren't, he wouldn't overwork them and would get them handicapped for future races before they realised what was going on. That way, the horses could not only start to win races at a more suitable level, they would also be able to continue improving for a longer period of time.

Chris gave me a few goes on Counsel's Opinion, one of those middle-distance handicappers who was on the cusp of Group level, and he was probably the first higher-class horse I had ever ridden. I started picking up a few better winners, but when there were so many other good jockeys around it really was difficult to start making an impact on the bigger stage. Perhaps the best illustration of this is that my first Group winner – the most important races that everyone aims for – came almost eight years after my first winner of any sort.

Wake Up Maggie had originally been Alan Munro's ride. She had been a very smart two-year-old who won a big sales race at the Curragh and in 2005 had finished second in the Group 1 Cheveley Park Stakes. Chris had hoped at one stage that she might have been a 1,000 Guineas filly, but things hadn't gone right in some way or other and she had been a little disappointing as a three-year-old. The owners had kept her in training at four, and although Alan was on the sidelines for medical reasons at the time, she had begun to look a bit more like her old self under several different jockeys.

One morning I reported for duty with Chris on the Newmarket

gallops and he suddenly said, 'You're getting on Wake Up Maggie today.' I remember thinking it was a bit unusual, as I'd seen her around the place but had never been asked to sit on her before. Instantly curious, I asked Chris what was going on. He replied, 'You're riding her at Glorious Goodwood.'

She was entered in the Group 3 Oak Tree Stakes and, honestly, it was the most excited I had ever felt getting on a horse. At the time, an 11-1 chance was a fancied ride for me in any Group race, let alone at one of the most important meetings of the year.

Wake Up Maggie was a filly who had her own ways of doing things, and it never helped if she was in front for too long. Chris had told me to be confident on her, so I kept her in behind, sneaked through fairly late and put her in front in the last 50 yards. In a big field it was quite a ballsy thing to do. What made it especially good was that I had beaten Richard Hughes in a tight finish in just the same sort of cheeky way that he would win time after time. I'd had my moments, but before this the only time I had ridden Group winners was on G1 Jockey, the racing game on my PlayStation.

You need those moments to act as turning points in your career. I had been riding for quite a while and always thought I could operate at a good level, so this was the proof. Group 3s aren't Group 1s, but at the time it was a seriously big deal for me. You always see a lot of jockeys chipping away and feel they must be doing fine – then you realise they haven't really ridden Group winners. Sometimes that never changes throughout their careers. I'd shown the confidence to hold my nerve on what was by quite a way Chris's best horse, and I hadn't messed it up for him.

Chris also trained a horse who I have probably been closer to than any other, given that he still lives in a field about five minutes from my house.

I rode Premio Loco on his first-ever run at Wolverhampton late in 2006. He was quite a backward sort of two-year-old and was actually well beaten as a 66-1 chance that day, but I remember, unusually for me, being particularly positive and keen on him when I gave Chris the debrief. I told him I thought he had run encouragingly for a long way, and that when he had been given some more time to strengthen up we might have a very nice horse on our hands.

That maiden at Wolverhampton turned out to have been quite a decent contest as the winner was Phoenix Tower, who finished second in four consecutive Group 1s for Sir Henry Cecil, and Premio Loco did go from strength to strength. The following spring under Ian Mongan he won very easily at Lingfield from Muhannak, who went on to win a Breeders' Cup Marathon, and throughout the next couple of seasons made really good progress without Chris wanting to get to the bottom of him. We were a good fit, as Premio Loco liked to have cover in a race, and that suited my patient style of riding.

By the start of 2009 he had become a Listed race winner on the all-weather at Kempton, and was such a promising new kid on the block that he was made hot favourite for Lingfield's Winter Derby. Sadly the day was not my finest hour, by some way.

I knew Lingfield like the back of my hand and decided to go around the field on the home bend to get a run, which on the surface the track had back then was usually possible. Unfortunately the gamble failed: I ended up giving away quite a lot of ground to my rivals, still got to the front too soon, and was beaten by Scintillo in a tight finish. It was probably the most angry I had ever been with myself over a ride as I felt it was my fault he had been beaten. It was before Premio Loco had actually become a serious Group horse, and three years later we did make amends in the same race, but at the time it felt as if he was my big chance of getting on a good one, and I might well have fucked it up.

Luckily both his owner Bernie Westley and Chris are very loyal, and they didn't need to say anything when I came back in. They could see how I felt, and whilst I didn't exactly tell them it had been completely horrific, I explained that if I had my time again I would definitely have done it slightly differently.

Thankfully it wa]sn't make or break for our partnership. In Baden-Baden in Germany that September, Premio Loco gave me my first Group 2 win, and a few weeks afterwards added another one in Cologne. The old boy seemed to enjoy the international travel, and on a later occasion we won the Pramms Memorial, Malmo's big international dirt race, which earned me lots of new contacts in Sweden. He's a horse who really did help me out in so many ways.

It's not uncommon for overseas riders to be brought across for the important races in Scandinavia, usually on Sundays during the summer months. My biggest supporter became Hans Adielsson, a top trainer of both trotters and thoroughbreds, who coincidentally had actually spent a little while training in Kingston Lisle for Beauchamp Magic's old owner Erik Penser. Hans ended up asking me to come across quite frequently for the better meetings. He would pick me up from the airport and he and his wife would often put me up at their house overnight if the racing went on late and I couldn't get home.

Riding at the dirt track at Jägersro was a completely different way of riding. It's very important to get a position from the gate and stay out of the kickback. Sweden did have the turf courses in Stockholm too: the old Täby track, and then the brand-new Bro Park just outside the capital. I actually won the Swedish 1,000 Guineas for Hans one year, but I'm not sure it really counts as a proper Classic – certainly when I got back to riding in England the next day no one in the weighing room knew about it!

Sweden is a strange country to ride in, as they don't have valets, so you have to organise all your own stuff. Sometimes you'll only have 20 minutes between races, rather than the 30 or 35 you get elsewhere, and if you have a handful of rides you have to sort all of your weights beforehand. On the other hand, you're allowed to take the saddle back into the weighing room for the trainer to come and get it. That would never happen in England, where they'd worry you were going to tamper with it.

In some respects the Swedes are more relaxed than us, but they aren't when it comes to the whip. You can only hit the horse three times, compared with the maximum of seven introduced in England back in 2011. If you go over the limit you get massive bans and can even be disqualified, so you've simply got to abide by the law.

When it comes to stricter rules it's similar in France: if you interfere with another horse, the stewards will normally amend the result so you are placed behind it. In approaching a race you have to have a different mindset, as you won't get away with some of the minor transgressions you'd get away with in England. Horses tend to stay straight more in France, because jockeys know that if they bump something else, there's always a chance they'll lose the race. I don't really agree with the rules – I prefer it if you can be a bit more aggressive – but it makes for cleaner racing.

Some of those overseas trips were worth it on a weekend if there was nothing to miss at home, as there was good prize money to be had and there would often be appearance payments on top. At one stage John Reid used to go across to Germany nearly every Sunday, as he had an agreement with an owner, and I am sure the trip was more than worth its while. Perhaps if the money had been such a fortune for me, I'd have done it as frequently as John, but on Sundays in recent years our domestic racing has steadily built up, and it wasn't really worth letting down anyone I rode for every other day of the week.

Premio Loco was rated 119 at his peak – a very solid Group 2 standard horse – but it made me realise there's still a bit of a gap from that sort of level to a Group 1, especially when he was running in the same era as the mighty Frankel. He did run well in a Lockinge and a Sussex Stakes, and took me to Royal Ascot for the Queen Anne Stakes, but to be really competitive there you have to be capable of stepping up another notch. Unfortunately, you don't really find bad Group 1s over a mile anywhere in the world – if he had been a mile-and-a-half horse, we would surely have plotted our way to one of the more winnable prizes somewhere around the world.

Our connection did get me out to Dubai a couple of times, and Premio Loco ran very well to finish fourth in the Godolphin Mile, one of the big all-weather races on World Cup night. Bernie very kindly said he would take us all out to a smart restaurant, and the booze flowed. Unfortunately, at some point in the evening the old drunken George must have decided to make an appearance and, while the whole thing was supposed to be Bernie's treat, I must have insisted on paying the bill. At one stage bottles of champagne had been ordered, though I have no memory of it, and given how expensive alcohol is in Dubai, it was quite a rude awakening the next morning when I looked at my credit card receipt.

It was in another race at Ascot, the Summer Mile, that I produced one of my most daring, or some might say reckless, rides on Premio Loco. We were one of the favourites for this Group 2 race, as Premio Loco had recently enjoyed a confidence-boosting win at Newmarket, and as we moved into contention everything seemed to be going smoothly.

With about a furlong left, I was looking to make a winning move, and had angled him up the far rail to find an opening inside Frankie Dettori and Forgotten Voice, who had been in the lead. If I say there was half a gap there, there wasn't really, but me being young and very enthusiastic, and Premio Loco being very willing, I shoved him into it. It was so tight that we actually bent the rail inwards and wiped Frankie out, causing him to stop riding, but we ploughed on through and won. I discovered later I had been hopping off the rail so much that I had actually ripped a hole in my boot.

When I walked back into the weighing room, Tony Culhane, a very experienced jockey, came up to me and shook my hand. 'That was a brilliant ride,' he said laughing, 'but you're gonna get four days for it!'

Tony was absolutely right, and although Frankie wasn't particularly pleased to have had his chance taken away, he was a gentleman about it. It is an unwritten rule in the weighing room that you don't get a fellow jockey in trouble with the stewards unless it's absolutely necessary, and whilst at the time, I imagine, he was wondering what on earth some idiot was doing, when we were taken into the stewards' room he helped me try and escape further punishment by telling them that he believed there'd been enough of an opening for me to get through.

The reason I got through that gap is because Premio Loco was so brave. It's a weird thing, but he was a horse who actually wanted to win, and I think that only a very small percentage of horses really want to do that. It's hard to put a figure on it – perhaps less than 10% – but if you watch most horses, they'll do everything they can to get out of winning. They might do the business now and then, or just win because they were a lot better than the rest, but there are few consistent triers. One time in the Celebration Mile at Goodwood, Premio Loco was leading, then looked as if he was beaten, and finally battled back to put his head in front again on the line. Certain horses just do that, not because I did anything special, but because they are willing to go through the pain barrier.

I don't mean that 90 per cent of horses absolutely don't want to win, but I think that the majority of them are just happy following the rest of the pack. That ten per cent are the ones who will actively help you out to finish first. Of course they don't know where the winning post is so the jockey's role is to get them to try their hardest as they approach it.

You often hear a line in racing about horses 'giving you everything', and with Premio it was almost to an extreme. He would lay it all down and give everything every time you asked, and there was never any doubt. You can sense it when you're riding a horse like that: you get a feeling when they drop their head and knuckle down. You're not trying to make a horse give you something they don't want to give.

I suspect that most horses are giving you 90 per cent of what they've got, and are always keeping ten per cent back for themselves. They're still working hard, and will be blowing after the race, but it's the jockey's job to try to eke that little bit more out of them.

I had a very interesting discussion with Harry Charlton, Roger's son and assistant, about measuring horses' heart rates. Monitors can give you an idea of what a heart rate can be pushed to, and it was quite interesting seeing how many won't push themselves right to that limit. There's a maximum rate, and some horses will always stay within that. I'm sure that some horses reach that limit and then won't do it again. I remember riding a few fillies that I felt had given me everything to win one day and wouldn't want to go back to that pain threshold again. I can understand why as it's clearly physical and psychological.

I could never work out why Premio Loco was quite so brave. Nicola looked after him in his retirement and she says that he's the thickest horse she's met in her life, so perhaps that's the key. He's very stubborn, and if he sets his mind to something he will do it, no matter what. Even if you've put his feed down directly in front of him, he'll still walk all around the stables looking everywhere else for it. He quite enjoys jumping and being hacked out by Nicola, who hopes to continue riding him and maybe doing a few little shows. When I had my accident, it was too much for her to continue organising him in the mornings as well as helping me, so the National Horseracing Museum in Newmarket very kindly stepped in. The museum has some beautifully restored boxes where the public can come and meet a few retired racehorses, and Premio Loco stayed there for a few months before he came back to us. The sweetest thing was that Billy Lord, who adored him when he used to look after him and ride him out when he was in training at Chris's, came and visited him nearly every day. I think they pretty much gave Billy his own set of keys.

Premio (Nicola does sometimes call him a bit worse when he's having one of his thick moments) is still a dude to have around: a very straightforward, happy chestnut. It sounds strange, but I put a lot of my success later on down to him. He was the first consistent big-league 'Saturday' horse I'd ridden, and we won 11 times – six at Group level – from 38 outings and collected more than £500,000 in prize funds. I always felt I owed him a lot, which is why, after partnering him in his final race at the end of 2014, I asked Bernie and Chris if I could have him. Now I'm slowly giving him back all the money we won as his food.

My strengthening ties with Gary Moore began at about the same time I was rising through the ranks with Chris. Gary is now the head of one of the great racing families: his late father Charlie was a real character who sold cars before becoming a trainer just down the road from Brighton racecourse. Gary was first a jump jockey around the Southern tracks before taking the stable over himself. His wife Jayne is an integral part of their operation and his children Ryan, Jamie, Josh and Hayley have all made it as riders.

Ryan is a year younger than me so he started to get going only a little while after I did. He, of course, has become perhaps the best Flat jockey in the world, and it quickly reached the point where he was in great demand with many of the top stables. That meant Gary needed someone else for his day-to-day stuff. He'd seen me riding, and was evidently impressed enough to get in touch. There wasn't an audition, and throughout my career I would pretty much ride all of his horses, unless Ryan happened to be available. It worked for all of us. I believe I rode 200 winners for Gary, which is an awful lot when you consider he splits his stable around half and half between the Flat and jumps horses.

Gary must be as good a dual-purpose trainer as there is. He's also incredibly hard-working, spending all available hours around his yard, and is a realistic, straightforward guy who has just about seen it all. We were honest with each other from the outset and, just as he appreciated my feedback, so I appreciated the way he trusted me to ride the races in the way I wanted: it just worked as a partnership. He was able to move from Brighton to an impressive stable near Horsham, and the quality of his horses continues to rise.

I was very rarely required to ride out for Gary, but he tells a good story about a time I popped by the yard on my way to racing at Brighton.

Someone had brought in some cupcakes and Gary asked me if I wanted one. As I took the rice paper off one of them I told him that was all I could afford to eat that day. Not much surprises Gary, but I think even he was fairly taken aback at how much I had to limit myself.

Gary would certainly let you know if you messed up, but he was not one for bollockings. It's a bit of a strange coincidence, but one of the only times we ever had any sort of disagreement was over the last horse I ever rode on a racecourse in England.

Etaad will not be remembered as the best horse Sheikh Hamdan Al Maktoum's Shadwell operation will ever breed, and he had ended up with Gary as a moderate all-weather horse. A few weeks before my accident I had been well beaten on him at Lingfield when he was a well-fancied 6-4 favourite. We were out the back the whole way: hardly the sort of result that pleases trainers or punters. Gary said he thought the horse had taken the mickey out of me, so I replied that I would get even with him. A week later I won on him at the same course.

Gary has a very dry sense of humour, too. One Monday night he had booked me to ride one of his in the last race at Windsor. It was my only ride at the meeting – Ryan had been at Windsor too, but for some reason wasn't riding this horse, and was finishing up and leaving the weighing room around the same time I was arriving. He had a bit of useful information up his sleeve. 'I haven't done it all day because I haven't been able to,' he said, 'but they've all been coming down the far side, and the best ground is on the stands rail.'

In the weighing room, Ryan would be quite a different character from the one you might see from the outside, when he's usually pretty serious and focused. He has an important job to do, so that's not surprising, but around fellow jockeys he never, ever comes across as grumpy. He's simply one of the lads – he's actually quite light-hearted and doesn't take himself too seriously.

And when it comes to tactics and getting an edge he's also incredibly switched on. Ryan suggested I tell his father that I would try and take this horse alone down by the stands on what would be a fresh strip of ground, and therefore an enormous advantage over our rivals. So I rang Gary and explained the plan.

'Well,' he said, 'if God says do it, then you'd better do it.'

I did what Ryan advised and the horse finished tailed off. When I spoke to Gary again after the race, he said in his typically understated way, 'God wasn't right this time, then.'

One of Chris's sayings was always, 'If things don't go right, there's always another day.' It's actually quite a big statement – if you're going to continue making your living as a jockey, you need to get it right more often than not – but it gave me a lot of confidence. Rather than trying to make things happen, you are better allowing the race to develop in front of you. Chris might sometimes point out a particular horse he thought might lead, or if there was going to be no pace at all, but the rest he would leave up to me.

Gary was much the same, and I do think the better trainers give you the belief to trust your own judgement, as more often than not you'll get a break at some time during a race. And they too know that even 'God' messes up sometimes.

CHAPTER SEVEN
A BREAK AT BECKHAMPTON

There are few attractions greater than the local trainer who has classic winners. For me that was Roger Charlton who took both the French and Irish Derbies in his very first season. He trained close to where I had grown up, my uncle Jerry had worked for a long time as his farrier, and I had always been interested in his horses. To be honest I had always been a little obsessed with getting an opportunity to ride for him.

Roger's red-brick Beckhampton stables, close to the Avebury stone circles, has two centuries' worth of history and was home to the training legends Fred Darling, Sir Noel Murless and Jeremy Tree, producing heaps of Classic winners. When you drive past the wide-open gallops on the road to Calne, it always looks amazing. Weirdly, even though I didn't know Roger at all, I had always imagined it being the place where I would end up.

Somehow Roger didn't quite share this glorious vision of my future. Every February or March before a new season, Guy or I would ring him up, or try his secretary, and neither an indication of interest nor even a returned call would be forthcoming. Roger was the biggest trainer in the area and a bit of a closed shop for outside riders. He had Steve Drowne as his stable jockey and Richard Hughes was retained for the horses that were owned by Juddmonte Farms, so he didn't really need anyone else coming in to help. He's not the sort of guy who would have people in there for the sake of it, and I would imagine he has loads of hungry young jockeys ringing him up every year asking for the same thing.

It was probably for four or five years before he finally said yes and I started going in there to ride out one day a week. I don't quite know why he eventually decided to give me a chance, but I had done myself a big favour when riding a sprinter of his called Genki. It was

Northumberland Plate Day at Newcastle in 2011, an afternoon when there are always loads of meetings on, and when Guy and I looked at the cards and saw he was entered, we were pretty sure Drownie would not go all the way up there for just one ride. Genki was quite fancied in the Group 3 Chipchase Stakes but he was a serial placer rather than a winner and a horse that you could never fully trust: he was one of those who needed kid-glove treatment. But on this occasion everything worked out perfectly. He didn't hit the front until late on and just beat Doncaster Rover in a tight finish.

I'd thought it was a normal kind of ride, but straight away Richard Mullen came over in the weighing room, put his arm around me and said, 'You were brilliant!' He might have used a stronger adjective than that, too, and as I watched the replay, I thought, 'Actually, I was quite good on that...'

I doubt whether it made a big difference to Roger, but it felt quite a significant moment for me – riding a Group winner for a big trainer – and it seemed to get the ball rolling. I got to keep the ride on Genki, who reverted to his usual habit of picking up the bits and pieces of place money in big races, finishing fourth in that year's Prix Maurice de Gheest at Deauville and in the Sprint Cup at Haydock. We never managed to win another race together, but on my part it wasn't through lack of trying.

I had ridden some decent horses for the likes of Chris Wall, but this was the first time I was consistently riding well-bred, proper horses at home. I had also never really been involved in a 100-plus-horse yard before.

If you didn't know Roger, I suppose he could come across as even a bit scary. He spent 12 years as assistant to Jeremy Tree, who trained many of Prince Khalid Abdullah's brilliant Juddmonte horses, before taking over at Beckhampton in 1990 and winning the English and

French Derby in his first season. He has produced some superstars over the years, like Tamarisk and Cityscape, and I was fortunate to arrive at a time when the stable had some great talents once again.

Roger leads by example, and is always very calm and collected – not a man to lose the plot and start shouting and screaming – but I think if he wasn't happy, you might feel pretty intimidated by him. He would generally keep his thoughts to himself, but if you made a massive mistake, you'd have a quiet chat about it. He's not someone who would say, 'My God, you were amazing!' but he would always say well done if you rode him a winner, and you felt that if you got some praise from him, you had definitely done a good job.

At heart, he's a man who is comfortable in his own skin, and believes in his own methods. He's confident enough not to worry about how well someone else might do with his horses if they were taken away from him. He just doesn't want any bullshit: he wants to know what you actually think about a horse rather than sugar-coating it. If you didn't rate a horse you had ridden one morning, you were far better simply telling him, 'I think this might just win a 0-65 handicap somewhere,' rather than, 'Well, if we get everything right he might end up being a 75-rated horse.' That way, if I thought I'd got a race wrong, I'd just tell him straight rather than make excuses or make out that it wasn't my fault. I would say I had learned something, and next time I would try something different. I think that's why we always got on quite well.

I'd certainly have liked to have had a contract with him, but it was always just a gentlemen's agreement. When I first arrived, he said I could come and ride work and, whilst there was no guarantee of any rides, he would try to help me out whenever he could. That's the way it always was. I knew some owners would want certain jockeys, and I would never have first call by any means, but it didn't matter. Roger likes team players – if you're on the team, he'll use you – but in return he expects loyalty. There is a core staff who have been there for a very long time, and I began to feel like a valued part of the set-up.

It was a privilege to ride work on some of the better horses, even if you knew it most likely they wouldn't be yours in a race. In 2012, James Doyle had broken onto the scene for Roger, particularly by winning easily on the Juddmonte-owned Cityscape in Dubai, and he was often the first choice. There was always the hope that you could pick up the occasional spares when others were not available, as I did on the top-class sprinter Bated Breath in the 2012 Temple Stakes at Haydock, before James got back on board to finish second in the King's Stand at Royal Ascot.

I think some people would get frustrated by only being a super-sub, but I would always try to see the bigger picture. If you think about it too much it'll just get to you. I knew I got more out of the situation with Roger than I was putting in, and I was probably never going to be his stable jockey anyway because I couldn't do very light weights. At least that helped me feel a bit better about it.

Anyway, as a rider it's quite special to get the chance to even sit on horses as good as Al Kazeem, Roger's multiple Group 1 winner. If there's one horse I'd have loved to have ridden in a race, though, it was Time Test. He might not have been an absolute superstar on the racecourse, and ended up finishing his career in America, but he was the best workhorse I ever sat on by a mile. He was an absolute machine.

Time Test and I ended up spending quite a lot of time together on the gallops, but it first came to my attention that he was quite good when someone else was riding him.

In 2015, Al Kazeem was being prepared for his first start of what was to be his final season, in the Prix d'Harcourt in France in early April. Perhaps ten days before the race we all went to Kempton for his last proper piece of work, and on this occasion I was given the leg-up. Al Kazeem had won the likes of the Eclipse and Prince of Wales's Stakes for James Doyle a couple of years earlier and had returned to Roger's care after proving subfertile as a stallion. He was never really flashy on the gallops and had got a bit more lethargic after his time at stud, but you would always describe him as a solid worker.

At Kempton, Al Kazeem felt as if he was working brilliantly, and we had zipped well clear of our lead horse. About half a furlong from the winning post, I decided to have a look behind to see where the third member of the party, Time Test, was. Willy Twiston-Davies was riding him, and I realised he was suddenly right on my quarters, absolutely pulling double, and could have passed me at any time.

At that stage, Time Test was only a young three-year-old, albeit one who had quite a big reputation at home. I imagine all the lads had been talking about him from the early days as he had been sent off at odds-on when he was beaten on his racecourse debut at two, and he was still considered an exciting prospect. I would never big horses up for no reason, but I remember saying to Roger, 'If I have ever seen Group 1 work, that's it.'

A little while later he ran in the London Gold Cup, a handicap at Newbury. I used to sit next to Ryan Moore in the weighing room, and at Newbury that day I said to him, 'If I have ever seen a certainty in my life, it's the horse you're riding in the next race' – and so it proved, as he won easily. A couple of months after that he went on to be a very impressive winner of the Tercentenary Stakes at Royal Ascot.

Time Test just had the most amazing cruising speed. It was almost like Usain Bolt at his best in the 100 metres, when it looked as if he was coasting and everyone else was struggling. He felt like he never came out of second gear. He would never be beaten by anything on the gallops, but for some reason he could never replicate it regularly on the track. There was obviously something not quite right with him, either mentally or physically. It was a shame, because some days he could be brilliant, but we never saw him achieve everything he was capable of.

James Doyle formally taking over as Juddmonte's retained rider did open up some more doors for me at Roger Charlton's, as it meant that sometimes James would be needed with other trainers for their horses. One occasion which worked out particularly well was when he had to go to France to ride Frankel's brother Noble Mission in the Grand Prix de Saint-Cloud in the summer of 2014. It meant there was a spare ride going on Thistle Bird, a filly I would not always have described in the same glowing terms as I would Time Test, in the Pretty Polly Stakes at the Curragh.

Thistle Bird belonged to Lady Rothschild, who must be the most enthusiastic owner-breeder ever. Not only does she love seeing her horses run, she also loves watching them work, and in the summer months she might come to Roger's once a week on a Wednesday to see them going out in the mornings. There were times she used to even pop in for evening stables too. Lady R just seemed to enjoy being at Beckhampton, taking in all the sights and sounds.

She knows the pedigrees of all her horses inside out. So I'll have to be kind to her in talking about Thistle Bird, who was certainly on the quirky side – you could probably even say she could be a bit of a madam. I had ridden her once before, when she had absolutely hacked up in a handicap at Windsor, but she had been through a stage of having to wear a hood to improve her concentration. First using the hood, and then later taking it off, transformed her from a handicapper into a Group horse, and it looked as if she might become a Group 1 winner one day.

Her chance finally came at the Curragh, and it was the easiest Group 1 winner anyone would ever ride. We had flown over in a jet from Farnborough airfield and the race just went perfectly. I tracked the leaders, sat in a nice position and only had to give her a couple of flicks of the whip to come cleanly away from Venus De Milo.

Lady R, who had come over for the race too, was absolutely thrilled, and it got me in her good books for a while. The greatest shame was that Thistle Bird had a recurring injury and never ran again. It wasn't the strongest fillies' division that season, and I'm confident that if she had remained sound she would have won a couple more Group 1s.

That year I also had a couple of chances on Al Kazeem, who was being brought slowly back to the boil after his disappointing adventure at stud. As he and James had been such a successful combination, Al Kazeem was his ride for the most part, but I stepped in to win the Winter Hill Stakes at Windsor in what was his second reappearance run. In early October, James had finished in mid-division on him in the Arc, probably the race I would most have loved to ride in, but when the horse was declared again for the Champion Stakes just 13 days later, he was claimed for Noble Mission and I got the call-up.

The pair of us were to be involved in a truly thrilling finish. James made the running, with me sitting just on his shoulder, and with two furlongs left we began to pull clear of the rest. It was a big ask for Al Kazeem to be at his best again in such a short space of time, but he gave me everything, drawing alongside Noble Mission only for James to squeeze out a little bit more from his horse and win by a neck.

It could have counted as frustrating to have finished such a close second in a huge race, but I preferred not to think of it in that way. Yes, I got beaten, and obviously I would rather have won, but it wasn't down to anything I did wrong. I was part of a great race and – I'm not just saying this out of politeness – I was genuinely delighted for James. He's a bit younger than me, but we had kind of grown up racing together, and were involved at a lot of the same yards. He's as lovely a fellow as he comes across. It's pretty widely known that there was a time when James thought he might be unable to carry on riding, and the knocks he has taken along the way mean he really appreciates everything he gets.

About this time, a certain horse called Quest For More was appearing on the scene, but if it had been down to me, he might have been plying his trade somewhere else rather than becoming a superstar who won Roger and me a Northumberland Plate, a Lonsdale Cup and a Prix du Cadran.

He was certainly a late developer. I had ridden him as a two-year-old and he was gradually coming along, but when we just about scraped home in the Gordon Carter Handicap at the end of his four-year-old season, I'd said to Roger that was maybe as good as he was, and perhaps it was time to move him on. It wasn't that I ever felt that he was ungenuine, but he was certainly slow, and perhaps that initially misled me into believing that he was keeping a bit to himself. Luckily his owner, Sultan Ahmad Shah, nearly always kept his horses in training, so it's pretty lucky that he didn't listen to me and sell him.

What we found Quest For More wanted was an extreme distance, and when he began to compete in the better staying races, he came into his own. He won a race at Goodwood the following season and Roger decided to run him in the Northumberland Plate. I don't think that we reckoned he was particularly well-handicapped to win such a competitive race, but he was clearly just getting better and better. That day he ended up carrying top weight to beat Willie Mullins' Max Dynamite and Nearly Caught in a performance that told us he was a Group horse. The following month he ran brilliantly in going down by a neck to Big Orange in the Goodwood Cup, and then went off to the Melbourne Cup where I would not have had a cat in hell's chance of making his scheduled weight of 8st 6lb, and Roger opted for the local knowledge of Australian jockey Damian Lane.

Whilst Roger was a wonderful man to work for, I think Quest For More played a part in perhaps the only time when there was any sort of tension in our relationship. This was shortly before he was due to run in the following year's Gold Cup at Royal Ascot. I had ridden for the stable in a race at Salisbury the week before, had been late finishing riding out and had to do 9st 5lb. There are a set of pads that Roger's stable like to use on their horses which have some non-slip mesh under them, and which maybe add 0.75lb of weight, whereas a normal light pad is 0.2lb. The horse was also owned by someone I hadn't ridden for before, and I wasn't aware that they only had a set of heavy colours.

I just couldn't do the weight using Roger's pad, so I just weighed out with a light pad. Roger must have heard about this, and on the Sunday morning before the Gold Cup he called me and said he wanted to have a chat about my weight. Straight away I shat myself and wondered where this was coming from. He asked me how it was, and I replied, fine. Then Roger said that when I was at Salisbury, it had seemed as though I was struggling to do 9st 5lb. I think I had to do 9st 2lb for Quest For More.

The Salisbury episode had been a case of me being a bit unprofessional and not managing my time properly, but Roger asked if I wondered whether my weight was becoming more of a problem than in previous years. It made me think, so I said if he was concerned about Quest For More and thought it was the right thing to do, then put someone else on him.

At that moment it felt like the right thing to say, but as soon as I'd hung the phone up I said to Nicola that I'd got the golf clubs in the car and would she drop me off at the course when she was heading out?

On the outskirts of Newbury there's a little nine-hole course called Deanwood, so I went to play a few holes on my own. All of the time it was grinding on me that I was about to give up my best ride of the year so easily. Quest For More would not have been favourite, but he would have been in there with a live chance on quick ground, and you don't get many opportunities to win a Gold Cup. I played four holes with it absolutely frying me that I hadn't even put up a fight. I had to ring Roger.

So I called him back straight away. 'You've known me long enough,' I said, 'and, to tell the tell truth, I am going to be strong enough doing 9st 2lb. I was having a bad day, and if you want to use a different jockey then that's fine, but don't worry, I'll definitely be able to do the job.'

In the end, Roger and I came to the conclusion this was a conversation we needed to have, but under different circumstances. He wanted to do his best by a horse with a serious chance, and was still worried that my weight was as bad as he'd seen. I'd dealt with the whole thing badly, but it made me realise that sometimes you've got to fight your corner and sort things out like men. Ironically, after all of that fuss, it rained at Ascot and Quest For More ended up not running – but Roger and I had straightened everything out with each other.

That October, shortly after I passed the post on Quest For More having won the Prix du Cadran, I got a pretty frank text message from Roger that went something like, 'I went off to make myself a cup of tea at halfway because I wondered what the fuck you were doing.' Since Roger's recollections of the race are a bit different to mine, we asked him to talk us through it for this book.

I had talked to George before the race. He had taken the view that Hughie Morrison had Nearly Caught in there, one of a couple of possible front-runners, so I said I would presume he'd go forwards and, if they were not going fast enough, he would make the running.

The stalls opened, and the horse sort of dropped out of

them, and was at the back of the field. I thought to myself, 'For God's sake, George – you must be asleep!' As it's a very long race, you get to walk around the kitchen about four times, and all the time I was thinking, 'Waste of time, waste of time...'

Then, miraculously, he came down the middle of the track and just got up to beat a pretty good horse in Vazirabad by a short neck.

It was just epic timing. He challenged wide on purpose and didn't help the other horse, who didn't want to be in front too long. It was the only time I think I ever thought he'd really fouled up, and while you don't mind in a little handicap, you do mind in a Group 1. Afterwards, George just said that he wouldn't go, and he had another way he could be ridden. He struck up a really good relationship with Quest For More, and won races on him that other people wouldn't have won.

I'd always rather Roger told it to me straight, rather than just saying, 'You were amazing...'

The race was actually a bit off the cuff. We did have a plan – Roger is quite calculated like that – but Quest For More just wasn't going in the first part of the race, and I wasn't quite sure why. But they were obviously going too quickly up front. He's the sort of horse that you never give up on, though, and whilst it might not have looked as if we were travelling all right, I kept hunting him along, as he was the strongest stayer I have ever ridden, and would have lasted four miles if I had needed him to.

When we turned into the straight they were stopping in front, but I was coming from so far back in the field that I couldn't see a passage through. Vazirabad had gone clear, so I had to switch wide, and that ended up being the best thing, as if I had challenged closer to Vazirabad it might have spurred him on. It proved that sometimes you just have to ride the race as it comes, and be prepared to change things if your plans go wrong.

I'd previously been placed in the Prix de l'Abbaye on the main weekend of racing in France, and it was such a great day to ride a winner at that meeting, even if it was on the Saturday before the Arc rather than the day itself. When you go to France normally, there's no one there, and the racing takes place in near silence, but that afternoon it was jam-packed. Sometimes just being involved on those big days is as special as the races themselves.

Clearly plenty of other jockeys would have loved to work with Roger, not just for all of those fantastic horses, but because he was such a gentleman. One Sunday I was in the car with my mate Dominic Elsworth going down to Goodwood to ride in the jump jockeys' Flat race they have there. Unsurprisingly, given that Dom is the tightest man in the world and wanted to save money, I was driving, and Roger called me on the hands-free. I was riding a horse who was having his first run back after being off the track a little while, and Roger delivered his orders along the lines of, 'Ride him for luck, take your time, if it opens up and you get a clear run then great, he should run well, but if it doesn't then don't crucify him.' His main interest was simply that the horse had a nice first introduction back on the course.

Perhaps the jump trainers are far more specific with their instructions, because when we ended the call, Dom was dumbfounded. 'Oh my God, that is just dynamite!' he exclaimed. 'What a man to ride for he is – he's given you a free rein to ride a horse to the best of its ability!' I don't think he had ever heard a trainer giving someone such reasonable and patient orders. At least I knew how lucky landing the Charlton connection had proved to be.

CHAPTER EIGHT
THE SEAL OF APPROVAL

When you start delivering for one big league trainer, others start to trust you too. Once linked with Roger I began to get rides from Marcus Tregoning, Jeremy Noseda, William Haggas and even the renowned Sir Michael Stoute. But it was another of the top names in Newmarket, James Fanshawe, who finally ended my quest for a Group 1 winner, which took nearly as long again as it had to get off the mark for my very first success on Wake Up Maggie.

Champions Day at Ascot, the valuable end-of-season finale, was not the sort of occasion I would usually be heavily involved in, even if I might have rides here or there, but in 2013 it was to prove particularly eventful. I had started off the day in the worst possible way. I was riding a horse called Harris Tweed for William Haggas in the Long Distance Cup, not one of the Group 1s, but still one of the important races on the card. He was a horse I got on well with, and I had given him every chance to win, but Johnny Murtagh got up and nutted me on the line with Royal Diamond.

When I walked back in, having blown a huge opportunity, I think it was as low as I have ever felt at the races. I remember thinking, 'Jesus Christ, what have I got to do to win one of these races?' I imagine I would have looked a bit dazed, but it was always my way to put on a bit of an act in the weighing room – the difficult thing about competitive sport is that amidst that kind of big-race atmosphere you can't just go and have a chat with your mates and say, 'I can't believe I got beaten on that!' I never wanted to betray any annoyance or disappointment, and preferred to deal with it internally. I went into the toilet, sat there for five minutes to gather my thoughts, and managed to put a brave face on it.

A few races later I had the mount on James Fanshawe's Seal Of Approval in the Fillies & Mares Stakes. Over the years, James Fanshawe had always been quite good to me, despite my not riding a lot for him, and in the early days I had won for him a few times on the smart sprinter Society Rock. He is a trainer that always gets the best out of his very good horses, and if I had ever lived in Newmarket permanently, I'm sure he's a trainer I would have tried to ride for a little bit more. If you want to make it as a jockey, Newmarket is the best place to be, but it never interested me. I'm Berkshire born and bred, and it suited to just drive there early in the morning if I was needed to ride out.

Seal Of Approval was really Hayley Turner's ride, but Hayley had been injured falling off her in the Park Hill Stakes at Doncaster a month earlier. As I had earlier deputised for Hayley in winning a Listed race at Newbury, she was handed back to me. Seal Of Approval was a 16-1 chance, the outsider of the whole field. We had hoped she would run well, but realistically the chance of me winning a race on Champions Day had probably gone. Incredibly, though, Seal Of Approval loved the soft ground that day, and ended up winning quite easily. I was quite overwhelmed, having gone from a massive low to a massive high in such a short space of time.

Nicola had come racing as well, more for just a nice day out than in the expectation of seeing me ride my first-ever Group 1 winner. Around the course I received so many congratulations – everyone seemed so happy for me. Perhaps because I didn't operate at that level very often, people made more of a big deal about it. I even remember Clare Hazell and Izzy Desailly, who worked for the Professional Jockeys Association, wanting to have a picture taken with me. It was so humbling to see people being genuinely happy for you. As I drove home in the car that night it didn't feel real. I was 31 years old, and it had taken me so long to get this far that sometimes I thought it was something that was never going to happen.

A lot of the prizes you get from winning races are quite ordinary.

You get a nice silver box from races at Royal Ascot, with the date on it, but most of the time you get a bit of glass or a picture frame. By the time you have 20 of those, the novelty has worn off, and I ended up giving most of them away. Luckily, I was given a really nice Qipco plate from Champions Day, something I will happily have on show.

There's not usually much time to celebrate a winner during the Flat season proper, as the racing never stops, and after Ascot I had to be in action at Bath on the Sunday. After racing at Bath I did manage to have an evening out with Jimmy Fortune, however, another jockey in the area who was good fun.

Things really were going along quite nicely in what were to be the final four years of my career. It wouldn't be a case of Guy Jewell hunting around for rides for me any more: they would come to him, and if a few different trainers were looking to book me for horses in the same race he might have to use his diplomacy.

I had also made an agreement to be jockey for Bjorn Nielsen, one of the country's most significant owner-breeders. Bjorn comes from South Africa, but lived in Epsom for a while in his youth and fell in love with the place. His big aim is one day to breed and own a Derby winner in his black and yellow silks. Bjorn has had horses with Roger for many years, and also owned Kingsdown Stables in Lambourn, where David Lanigan was based before Ed Walker moved in. His previous jockey Ted Durcan was developing closer ties with Sir Michael Stoute in Newmarket, and I believe it was Mikael Magnusson, a former trainer and one of Bjorn's good friends, who had suggested me for the role.

Perhaps for the only time in my career, I had access to beautifully bred horses which were just mine to ride, and it was a bit of extra security. Bjorn is a financial trader and spends most of his time in America, but he is hands-on as an owner, and every time I rode one of his horses I would ring him to keep him in the loop.

We didn't exactly have a golden run together, though. Winning the 2015 Wokingham at Royal Ascot with Inception would have been the highlight, and David trained a decent stayer for Bjorn called Biographer, but having quite a few of those later-developing horses can be a bit of a waiting game, and unfortunately you don't get superstars every season. The excitement was that, given the quality of animal he buys and breeds, there could always be the chance of a nice one coming through.

I suppose it would have been easy to have felt a little bitter or frustrated when a horse like Stradivarius came along when I was on the sidelines, and won not only at Royal Ascot but also the Goodwood Cup in 2017. But it's not like that at all. It wasn't something that was even up for discussion with Bjorn, as Stradivarius was trained by John Gosden, a man I only ever rode for a couple of times. Had I still been competing, I suppose there's a chance he might have been my ride, but it was an absolute thrill to be at Ascot a year later to see him starring in a fantastic Gold Cup.

I loved going to Kingsdown and built up a good friendship with Ed Walker, a young trainer going places, and Bjorn continues to be very supportive. There's no point thinking about the ifs and buts – you've got to move on – and I would like nothing more than for him to win the Derby. It's a nearly impossible dream, but he'll keep going at it.

This added stability meant I didn't always have to be flat out the whole time. Nicola and I were able to take a couple of weeks' holiday every so often, and in December or January we would go off somewhere warm like Barbados, Egypt or Cuba and recharge the batteries. I couldn't afford to come back weighing 12 stone or something and find I wasn't able to shift it, but for the first half of these holidays I would totally pig out, and eat and drink anything I wanted. Once I was satisfied, I would just try to be a little healthier in the second week. A switch-off like this was just as helpful for Nicola from her long days in the yard – generally staff members get one and a half days off every two weeks, and that's a pretty hardcore work schedule.

I wouldn't get the post-holiday blues when I went back to the winter all-weather circuit, as I never found going racing boring. Sure, you have those times when it's just another day at the office, but I always tried to appreciate that I was being paid to indulge my hobby. Towards the end it was a bit of a relief that I rarely had to make the long journey up to Southwell unless I absolutely had to, as the racing there tended to be very moderate, and Guy and I decided it wasn't really worth my time. I could keep a couple of pounds heavier in the winter, so that I felt a bit better, and wouldn't do very light at all – maybe 9st 3lb or 9st 4lb at a push if a really good chance came along.

I don't think it ever got physically problematic to actually lose the weight, but you must have the motivation. You'd find it easy enough to get down to 9st 1lb if it was to ride a Harris Tweed or a Seal Of Approval in a big race – when your head is turned by the bigger occasions you can become a bit of a racing snob – but when you think, 'This horse just can't win, no matter what weight I do on it,' it's hard to go and sit in the bath to drop 4lb.

I sat talking about this in the weighing room one day with Adam Kirby, who is not only tall like me but followed the same sort of career path: from breaking through from a low level and excelling on the all-weather to getting better chances later on. When you're skint, the one thing that drives you on is earning enough to pay your bills, but Adam and I agreed that once you get beyond that you need a couple of nicer horses on the boil to get you through those long, cold winters on the all-weather. They didn't have to be the next Frankel, just something you could look forward to winning a decent race in the summer on.

There were always peaks and troughs. For many years Gary Moore had been my biggest supplier of winners in the winter, and when I started riding for him, I'd be cleaning up almost every week. But Gary had started to have some significant success over jumps, through the likes of his Queen Mother Champion Chase star Sire De Grugy, and now decided to concentrate more on that side of the game. I owe Gary a lot, and would never blame him for doing that – you've got to take success when and where you can.

My annual number of winners towards the end was no different to what it had been in earlier seasons, and I'm sure most people would have wondered why I was moaning about something so trivial, but I was definitely a diminishing force on the all-weather. I didn't really ride for Godolphin, who were starting to mop up a lot of the races, and I had a little less firepower. As much as I've said that I'd started to pick and choose, and was not desperate to be the all-weather champion jockey, I kind of needed to be busy to keep my weight in order. I'd also always be aiming to reach a century of winners during the year. To do that, you've got to hit the ground running, and you simply can't afford a couple of quiet months.

I probably wanted it both ways, but that's what happens when you're obsessed with winning and living inside that bubble. Silly things niggled at me. When Ed moved to Kingsdown from Newmarket at the end of 2016, he decided to have a team for the all-weather, so he'd have a few horses to get to know the new gallops with. He had Tom Brown in the yard to ride out for him every day, and I noticed he was beginning to pick up quite a few winners. As I rode for Ed a lot on grass, I started wondering whether I should ask him if I could come and ride out during the winter too. The flip side, of course, is that I would be taking away from Tom what he'd been grafting so hard for. Ed had never realised I'd be thinking like that, but I was so greedy that seeing horses winning that you felt you should be riding got to me.

This all sounds as if I'd turned into a right big-time Charlie after winning a few decent races, but it was just one of those periods when you've got to ride the storm and keep kicking.

At least being more sensible meant I was in a very good way physically. For many years my long-term view was that I would be able to continue riding until I was 35. By the time of my final ride I was 34, and I genuinely felt I was in the sort of place where I'd have been able to go on a fair way further. From time to time Guy and I would discuss things, and at one early stage we loosely talked about my going on until I was 40, and later it moved to until Guy himself wanted to retire. The goalposts were moving naturally and by the end of my career, I felt so good that I'm sure that I could have gone on until I was 50. Perhaps it would have got harder to do the weights as I got that little bit older, but I certainly wasn't short of motivation to keep myself in shape.

CHAPTER NINE
SECRETS TO SUCCESS

What does it take to make a good jockey? I've thought about it a lot over the years. Some of it is undoubtedly down to talent and lucky breaks, but when I was younger and starting to do well, I would always be watching the best riders in the weighing room, trying to learn from how they conducted themselves both in and out of the saddle.

Someone who particularly interested me was Ray Cochrane – a man I didn't know well in those days and still don't. He was the full package. He had great hands and was very easy to watch, but above all he never looked like anything ever bothered him. When you watch the best jockeys ride, you never think, 'My God, what are you doing?' It's easy viewing. Ray kept things straightforward and didn't really mess up. Even if they're slightly out of position in a race, it always looks as if the top guys aren't about to start panicking or doing something rash.

Ray was a proper tough, hardy guy who had won the Derby in the late eighties, and although I wouldn't exactly say everyone was running scared of him, he was clearly in charge. I thought that even if I wasn't quite like that, I'd got to start putting a bit of a front on. Ray was obviously a very successful jockey, and I've seen lots more since then, and nothing seems to faze them. They never look like they're weak. If people could see your weakness, I always felt, it was to their advantage.

The best jockeys are able to deal with defeat well. When you get beaten on something you shouldn't have been beaten on, if you then hold on to that losing feeling it's bound to affect your future rides. You've simply got to work out what you've done wrong, and drop it. On a few occasions when I thought I'd given horses stinkers, often rides that wouldn't have been mentioned in the paper or debated about on TV, I'd get home, watch the replay, then forget about it. In the weighing room you can see who can deal with disappointment and who can't, and some jockeys can be so intense, even haunted by defeat. Even something very minor might affect them for weeks and weeks.

When I was younger I used to love watching Frankie Dettori. It always looked so easy for him. But times change, and I'll never forget seeing him one afternoon at Sandown. He had lost his job with Godolphin and had said he was going to re-establish himself and try to win the title. Unfortunately Frankie was on a seriously bad run: it was horrific – he'd ridden only a handful of winners all year and had come along on the day for a few rides on no-hopers. I was sitting quietly in the corner of the weighing room as usual, and he just looked a broken man. Everyone knows Frankie is a showman, and normally he's full of beans, a good, fun guy to have around who doesn't get too tense. You'd never think you'd see Frankie Dettori down in the dumps like that ever, even if he could still put on a front for the cameras. When you see someone who's been at the highest level back down at the bottom, it makes you realise no one is invincible.

It's funny how it goes, though. It wasn't long afterwards that he was back riding top horses for John Gosden, and had turned the corner.

Experience is vital, too. I can't stand it when there's a promising new apprentice on the scene and everyone has decided that they're so good. If you have too much success too early it can be more of a hindrance than a help: you think you've made it, maybe get big-headed and don't allow yourself to be open to improving. You see many jockeys who are a big hit as a kid fall off the wagon.

One thing Mark Usher instilled in me from a young age is not to bully horses. You've got to leave them alone if you can: it's much easier to get horses to do stuff if they want to do it, rather than try to make them. When I was starting out, Kieren Fallon was on a massive high. You'd often hear people saying that 'Kieren lifted that one home', implying that the force of the jockey was the reason his horse had won a race. You realise after riding for a long time that this can't be correct. Don't get me wrong: a jockey can make a difference, but the truth is that to be a good jockey, you've got to kid horses along, to get them to help you. I know it looks to the eye as if Tony McCoy has carried a horse around Cheltenham, but really he has kidded it along. It can seem as if it's all about the physical effort, but that's a bit of an illusion.

Not enough is made about getting a horse to relax. As soon as we'd leave the stalls, all that would concern me was to get my horse switched off and running as economically as possible. When you're tall it's probably easier, because you ride that little bit deeper, but I always felt it was one of my strong points. Even if the horse jumped out and was a bit keen or free-going, I would try not to touch it – almost trusting it to switch off itself. It is amazing how many horses will relax and get into a rhythm if you don't grab at them.

I can never understand it when jockeys insist on shoving along a horse that's keen to get it into the position they wanted to be in. It's only going to cause the horse to run with the choke out and exert itself too much. There are always exceptions to the rule when horses are keen and still win, but more often than not they don't, because they fold up more quickly.

When my height shot up, I found it more difficult to get my arse down in the saddle, and I had to really work hard to make myself look tidier and more competent. In my early days it was also more fashionable for jockeys to ride with a short stirrup length, almost perched up on top of the horse. Frankie Dettori does that, rides very short, but he's still so neat and tidy, and it helps that he's got the most amazing balance. I saw a picture of my first-ever double, for

Mark Brisbourne at Hamilton Park in May 2000, and it did look as if I rode short back then, but I just wasn't made to ride like that later on. I do feel that having a more sensible length made it easier to be in rhythm with the horse, anyway.

I was also quite particular about learning to flick my whip through to my other hand. I'm not ambidextrous by any means, but it would have been easy to have let my favoured right hand become dominant. You should have the whip in your outside hand, so if you're riding on a right-handed track, you want it in your left hand jumping out of the stalls. Otherwise, if the horse starts hanging away from the rail, as they often can, you'll waste time pulling the whip through in order to correct it. It doesn't feel natural to leave the stalls with the whip in your 'wrong' hand, but when the all-weather track was opened at Kempton, it was a huge help to be able to practise it all through the winter. You do need to switch the stick through from hand to hand during the race, and if you get in a muddle and it takes you a while, in a tight finish it can be the difference between winning and losing. I practised so much it almost became second nature.

There was another edge I had which probably fewer people noticed. It came from the spell I spent in Dubai as a teenager working for Godolphin's trainer Saeed Bin Suroor. His assistant, Tom Albertrani, was an important figure in the team at the time, and he was fanatical about making sure a horse changes its lead leg. He explained the process to me one morning, and it stuck with me throughout my career. Tom was an American, and it would have been considered particularly important on the tight dirt ovals where he came from.

The key part of his thinking was that you want the horse to have fresh legs. If a horse is leading with only its near fore (front left) leg all of the time, it is going to get tired on one side, so when you switch, it's like they get a new lease of life. When you go around a left-handed bend, you want the horse leading with its near fore, but then you would flick onto a fresh lead up the straight. Most horses will switch to the correct lead when going around a bend, but they won't always switch to the outside lead going out of the bend. It is very easy to get them to do it by just adjusting your weight and moving the horse maybe half a horse width off the bend. On a straight track such as Newmarket it would be just as important, as you conserved the horse's energy and kept it going in a rhythm. I would almost want it to change leads every two or three furlongs, so by the time you came to the finish it would be doing it consistently and not fighting you. When I was riding it was one of the most important things I'd do, and I believe it could make at least a length or two's difference in a race.

The key to riding in any race is always to make a plan. When I was doing my form, the day before or in the morning, I'd give myself various scenarios and work out how I might deal with them. It's never going to go according to the script all the time – you have to use a bit of feel and instinct – but you must always know about your opposition. For example, I would always like to be following a horse that could lead me to where I wanted to go. I could never understand when jockeys switched out and started following one that on form had no chance! Sure, 100-1 shots do win races sometimes, but you don't want to be following them. There's no excuse not to be clued up – it's so easy nowadays to pull up the replays. I imagine it would have been a lot harder without the internet, but even in a 16-runner race, I could usually get my form done within half an hour.

The other weird obsession I had was that even if I was riding in a race against a 1-5 shot that really shouldn't lose, I would always try and find some kind of weakness in the favourite and tell the trainer how I thought we could beat it. Obviously it didn't often work out, and it's OK to go down to the start thinking your horse has got no hope of winning, because very often it hasn't, but when it has something of a chance, you must always consider the possibilities. You see short-priced favourites getting turned over all the time, but if you go out with a negative mindset, it isn't going to help you.

I wouldn't say I was a 'Norm' who watched every single race every day, but I did find the form side of things interesting. It was also helpful to see how the handicapper had assessed horses and moved them up and down in the ratings. I might have won on a horse and looked as if I had ridden it right out to the finish, with the result that it would be raised a few pounds in the handicap. But in reality, I would have been the only one to know that the horse had actually won quite easily, and should have been given even more weight the next time.

Plenty of jockeys don't let on that they know what's going on. A lot of it is game-playing. Not much is discussed between jockeys before a race – down at the start you might get a good idea of who's going to make the running, but that's about it. If you're in a really good race, no one's going to let you know anything about their plans. But when you're riding against the same group of jockeys all the time, you get to know their styles. Some you might think are going well, and then when they come off the bridle and under pressure they find absolutely nothing.

One I'd find very hard to read when I started out was Kieren. He'd look as if he was hard at work, so you'd start thinking you'd need to get out of the way before he started going backwards – and the next minute, he'd won the race! Kieren would have a loose rein, but he was just humouring horses along. Richard Hughes was hard to gauge in the opposite way: he'd sit on fresh air. You'd be thinking he was cantering, so you'd stay in behind him, then he'd let the horse down and it would go nowhere. He'd almost get everything out of them without getting them off the bridle.

I learned my trade on the all-weather where momentum was everything, especially at Lingfield. If you got behind a horse that stopped in front of you, you'd probably have to stop riding and switch to get around them. And if you had to do that, you'd never win the race.

I'd like to think I was a useful asset to my trainers on the gallops as well as the racecourse, and one of my strengths was that I would never wear rose-tinted spectacles or tell a trainer their horse was a flying machine. For a horse to impress me, it would have to do a lot of things right, and I'd believe in my feel for them, knowing for example if one didn't want a level track or to run left-handed. I'd take everything into account in order to make a more accurate mental assessment. I'd think about the ground conditions; I'd make note of whether the lad riding my galloping companion was much heavier or lighter than I was, which would affect the merit of the performance. My parents even found notebooks I had filled with remarks I'd made about horses even going back to my time with Dermid and Mark, so I'd clearly been particular about making records for some time.

You also know as soon as you start working how the horse is blowing, so you can tell if it's finding things easy. Different gallops affect things too: I found it harder in Newmarket, as the famous Racecourse Side and Limekilns gallops are quite easy, and you can get lesser horses to work well on them. But if a horse worked well on the trial grounds, a tough grass gallop along the top of Roger's place at Beckhampton, then more often than not they were fairly decent. I'd work out a rating for a horse and then be able to tell a trainer it might not be good enough to win a maiden. It was better in the long term to be realistic.

Horses such as Time Test, however, can deceive you on the gallops. I remember a horse Chris Wall once took on called Habshan, who had been with Neil Graham and Michael Jarvis earlier in his career. Habshan was quite unreal on the gallops: he'd kick anything else Chris had into touch, and although he was only a handicapper rated in the 80s, he genuinely worked like a horse rated well over 100. I imagine rumours would get around of his exploits among the lads in Newmarket, and I remember him on one occasion being backed off the boards only to get beaten. A lad I knew in one of Habshan's previous stables told me the same thing had happened when he was with them. To be fair to Habshan, he won a few times, and Chris will have trained many worse horses, but I always found him very frustrating.

Some trainers are very particular about giving you tactics, but when you become relatively successful you're allowed more free rein. Towards the end, most would trust me to do what I thought was best, and Gary Moore would never tell me anything. Largely, he said, because I wouldn't have listened anyway!

It's a bit different when Sir Mark Prescott asks you to ride for him. Sir Mark, who is one of the sport's most engaging and popular figures, is a stickler for discipline. When he gets in touch with you, it's a bit like if you heard from the Queen. I only rode for him a few times, but on the first occasion I remember getting a message from his office saying he was going to ring at a particular time and to make sure I was around. Sure enough, I received a call from a withheld number. The race was at Lingfield, and Sir Mark said that when we passed the five-furlong chute, around four and a half furlongs from home, under all circumstances get the horse on the stretch, because it was slow and all it did was stay. Then, a day before the race, Seb Sanders, Sir Mark's stable jockey, came over to me in the weighing room with another reminder: 'Whatever you do, kick on with this horse a long way from home, because it takes ages to get going.'

I did what I was told, to the letter: went a couple of lengths clear and got caught late on. If I had done my own thing it would have won, definitely, but because you are riding for someone like Sir Mark, you follow orders. He was absolutely fine about it, and said he would never, ever be critical of a jockey if they did what they were told. 'I've learned something about the horse,' he said, 'and if you'd have taken your time it would have won.'

I imagine part of the reason Seb and Sir Mark had impressed upon me that I was to kick on soon was because of my reputation for being patient in behind and getting there late. In the press I was occasionally referred to as the 'head waiter', a nickname first given to Harry Wragg many years earlier. I suppose many trainers would expect me to do that, but I always believed I could tell if we were going too slowly or too quickly, and adjust tactics accordingly. I caught Chris Wall by complete surprise one day at Pontefract aboard a nice sprint filly of his called Bounty Box, who we usually held up, but when it became apparent at the start that nobody was going to make the running I changed things. We led nearly all of the way and kicked clear around the tight home bend, which was quite satisfying.

Sometimes I was pretty sure that the instructions I received from trainers were not going to make the horse win the race, so I disobeyed them. Unfortunately, altering tactics can cause riots and arguments if it doesn't work out, as you're the one in the firing line. More often than not, I'd get that sort of thing right, but I remember Milton Bradley, a veteran trainer, and I fell out big time. I was told to be handy at Wolverhampton one day, but the horse missed the break, and I would have had to gun it to get it back into a forward position. That wasn't really my style, so I left it alone and it ran pretty well to finish third. I actually thought I'd given the horse quite a good ride, but when I say they went mental, they went absolutely doolally. The girl who was leading the horse up started it off, and Milton continued it on the phone. We had to agree to disagree.

I generally tried not to burn any bridges, as you never know when you might need someone. And I should certainly have known better during the last full year of my career than to have had a petty disagreement with the local trainer Geoffrey Deacon.

At Lingfield one afternoon I was riding Glastonberry, a sweet grey mare I'd won a load of races on, and I had quite a good strike-rate on Geoffrey's other horses. I'd felt she was probably still on a high enough handicap mark and that things would need to go perfectly to win the race, so I dropped her out and came wide and late to finish fourth. I don't think Geoff was particularly happy with the ride, and when the owners were with us he said something about whether it might have been better to have switched Glastonberry the other way. Usually I would bite my tongue and maybe talk about it the next day when things had settled down, but this time, for some reason, I snapped. I gave him a look in the eye of no uncertain meaning and stormed off straight away like a moody teenager. It had only been Geoff's opinion, and he probably wasn't even being mean – at the time his horses hadn't been going great, and he'd have been under a fair bit of pressure from his owners to be doing better. Later we had a fairly heated conversation on the phone: I was still convinced he was wrong and I held the grudge for ages, refusing to ride for him when he called Guy to book me again.

If Roger Charlton had said something similar to me, there's no way I'd have behaved like that: I'd have been thinking about the bigger picture. But I'd have been of the opinion that Geoff, a smaller trainer without so many runners, would have needed me more than I needed him, and that was a really poor way of behaving.

I have also ridden for some quite big gambling owners over the years, and people always think of Gary as someone who lands touches. However, I can never, ever remember anyone to do with him putting any pressure on me to get it right. It was always just to think about how the race would unfold and come up with a plan.

The most successful gamblers never mention having had a bet beforehand, or really let on if they're annoyed about it afterwards if it goes wrong, as they know you're doing your best. If I made a mistake, I would always tell them and be quite critical of myself. That usually defuses a situation. A few times I only found out afterwards that an owner had absolutely lumped on, and sometimes when I had given the horse a ballsy ride. I suppose there's a chance I would have ridden it differently if I had known, so it's probably better to be ignorant.

One trainer who's probably glad to see the back of me is David Barron, the straight-talking Yorkshireman who is known as a pretty shrewd operator. As a 3lb claimer I once rode a horse of his called Charge, owned by the well-known gambling owner Nigel Shields, for whom I rode a few on the all-weather. We led until about a furlong to go at Lingfield, but were well beaten as a 2-1 favourite. I'd never dealt with Barron before, but when I called him after the race, he said, 'I'll give you one piece of advice. Ring up the Jockey Club, give your licence back and give up.'

Many years later, I rode for him again at Goodwood, and gave a horse a stones of a ride. He told me to get there late, but I just sat and waited and by the time I got out with about half a furlong left, I had no chance to win. About two weeks later I managed to win the Temple

Stakes on his star sprinter Pearl Secret, but I think that was more the owners Qatar Racing's decision than his. He probably felt he'd been lumbered with me again.

Racing is an opinion-based sport, which is why so many people love it, and everyone is entitled to their view. I should think any jockey who has a social media account is well aware of this. I used to use Twitter, and would get a bit of abuse, but I just ignored it. It's always the risk when you're holding a horse up and it gets beaten. People think you're overcomplicating things. Some jockeys reply to comments or get annoyed about them, but I was always pretty thick-skinned, even if I had cocked something up.

Far worse than Twitter was the old Betfair forum, a place where punters would get together on the betting exchange. Someone once mentioned it to me and I couldn't resist having a look. The abuse there was brutal, with people writing that they wished that you were dead. It's quite funny to start with, finding your name and seeing what people are saying about you, but no one ever praised a good ride: it was just abuse, and mostly people speaking through their pockets. Those that knew me know I was always doing my best, and all that stuff about 'He stopped that horse' was plain rubbish.

The only thing I found quite hard was coming in straight after a race where I'd maybe been a little unlucky or got something wrong, because I hadn't processed it yet. If you're walking back to the weighing room after getting off a horse and someone's going crazy at you and shouting, 'What the fuck were you playing at there?' it's hard not to get touchy about it. I remember I got beaten on one of Gary's at Brighton one day, and a bloke on the other side of the rail started shouting dog's abuse at me. In retrospect it was quite funny, as he wasn't a particularly big fellow and I lost the plot with him. Gary had to grab me and bundle me off.

Most of my friends would say I can be very stubborn – because I'm nearly always right, of course – and on the rare occasions when I lost my temper on the racecourse it was never half-measures. The trainer Ralph Beckett and I had something of a difference of opinion one afternoon about a race at Nottingham. Ralph had just employed Fran Berry as his stable jockey and I was on board one of Roger's in a minor race. Fran came upsides me and was trying to get out, but I just stood my ground and held him in. There was a stewards' inquiry afterwards, and I think Fran may have been cautioned for his ride, but when I got in the car to drive home there was a text message from Ralph saying something like, 'Thanks for all your help in the 2.35 at Nottingham, much appreciated.' I suspected he was just frustrated and having a bit of a dig, so I rang back straight away and completely lost it with him, basically calling him every name under the sun. I was convinced I was in the right and had been trying to win the race, and didn't exactly cost Ralph's horse its chance. It was just one of those silly things. I would still ride for Ralph from time to time, and after I had to retire he wrote me the most beautiful letter, which is the true measure of the man.

I may be stubborn but I can appreciate decent behaviour when I see it. A good jockey ought to be up for that.

CHAPTER TEN
A MODERN-DAY CLASSIC

The Classics are the flat race jockeys chance to write his name in history. The 2,000 Guineas, 1,000 Guineas, Derby, Oaks and St Leger are the five races that for 200 years have been the benchmark tests on which each generation is measured and for me, opportunities to ride in them were few and far between. Yet at my first attempt, on little Rising Cross in the 2006 Oaks, I actually finished an unexpected second.

Her trainer, John Best, had been a regular supporter of mine on the all-weather circuit for many years, but I'd only got the ride on his filly a month earlier after we had dead-heated with my good pal Dane O'Neill and Soft Centre in the Lupe Stakes at Goodwood, and he decided it was worth trying her at Epsom. Obviously it's exciting to be involved in the Oaks, but the expectations were that she was going in there as a 33-1 shot. Getting on a horse you know, if everything goes to plan, should win, and knowing that the trainer and owner have kept faith in you even when someone like Ryan Moore or Frankie Dettori is available, is when it really feels like a big deal. You do see some jockeys going out for a big race and clearly bricking it, and if you were on the favourite in the Derby the pressure might get to you, but that never came around, so I will never know how I would have dealt with it. I always believed in what I was doing and that I was good enough to do it, so I never really felt nervous walking out of the weighing room.

Anyway, Rising Cross ran really well, although I nearly fell off her when she stumbled with about a furlong to go. As she was so small and I was so tall, John joked that I had just put my foot on the floor and pushed her back up. Going down to Tattenham Corner there was a bit of excitement as she was travelling so nicely, but in behind me, and going an awful lot better, was Kieren Fallon and Alexandrova, who eventually won by six lengths. Rising Cross was a good filly if not an absolute superstar, and it was nice to have done well for her connections on the day on what was a huge occasion for John's small Kent stable, even if I can't pretend I was exactly living a high from the experience. She was only second, after all, and for a jockey second is nowhere.

After that, I rode Rising Cross in the Italian Oaks in Milan. It didn't go anything like as well, as I was basically a marked man on a hot favourite. I could hear a bit of shouting in the race, none of which I could understand, and some of the others made sure I was never in a position where I wanted to be, and we finished a disappointing eighth.

I had a couple of goes in the Guineas, but never the Derby. Late in my career I believe I got overlooked on a horse that I had ridden before, and which ended up running as an outsider. Perhaps I should have chased the ride harder, as it would have been a lovely thing to have achieved, but you can't magic Derby rides out of thin air. That particular horse wasn't always my ride, and it would have been far more frustrating if I had been riding one that was being prepared for Epsom all the way through, and then been taken off it.

Fortunately, I will always be able to say that I am a winner of the oldest Classic, the St Leger, far and away the biggest milestone in my racing life.

That meeting at Doncaster in September 2016 did not get off to a flyer. Actually, I would go as far as to describe it as an absolute nightmare. I was in action at the course on the Friday with what I felt was a pretty good book of rides, beginning with Brian Ellison's Seamour, who was quite well fancied in the Mallard Stakes after finishing fifth in the Ebor at York. However, it was not to be one of my finest hours in the saddle. I hadn't ridden Seamour before, but I'd seen him plenty of times and had done my homework. Brian just said to take my time before producing him with a run, but I kicked far too soon and ended up being caught and beaten by a horse of Hugo Palmer's called Wall Of Fire, who turned out to be quite decent later on. One of my greatest annoyances was going too soon on a horse, especially if it didn't do much in front. I'd even watched Seamour pulling up in front in the Northumberland Plate the year before, when Quest For More had gone past him. I remember thinking to myself, if I ever got a go on the horse another time, I wouldn't do that. And what had I bloody done? Exactly the same thing.

Then to make the cut even deeper, I was on Quest For More in the very next race, the Doncaster Cup. He was favourite after his good win in the Lonsdale Cup a few weeks earlier, and I decided to go for the same tactics and make all of the running. Questy ran a stonker of a race, leading for nearly every yard, only to get nutted on the line by Sheikhzayedroad.

There were no further opportunities to make amends that afternoon, and as much as I was nearly always a good loser, I was fuming about what should have been a significant big-race double on the eve of my first St Leger ride on Harbour Law.

Luckily I had organised to go and play a quick round of golf with Mick Fitzgerald, the former jump jockey who is now a television presenter. That got rid of some of the frustrations, and I later headed out for a spot of dinner at a Chinese restaurant nearby with the jockeys Jamie Spencer and Sean Levey and a friend of Jamie's who was working on the Channel 4 Racing production team.

I've always loved an overnight stay with the boys, as you get to spend time with people you wouldn't always see much socially. Everyone was in quite good spirits, and while I just managed to eat a bit of fish and didn't have a drink, it was just the job to take my mind off what had happened. Neither of the other two were riding in the Leger, so I don't think it was even mentioned. Conversation was the typical jockey stuff: failed marriages and so on.

I was staying at a Best Western hotel nearby, and as it was not a normal thing for me to be riding in a Classic, I decided I should have a quick look at the track first thing in the morning. I was eating an early breakfast on my own and found myself joined by the trainer Richard Hannon, who was running Ventura Storm in the Leger. Little did I know that in about eight hours' time it would be me who was denying Richard his big-race glory when Harbour Law would beat Ventura Storm to the post. Richard recognised the irony of this later and told the press after the race that he had bought me my breakfast to boot. I ought to just point out that this is a load of bollocks: breakfast was included on my room.

I left Richard at the hotel and went and power-walked down the track, finishing with plenty of time to spare. Harbour Law had 9st 1lb, my first ride of the day, and I had a perfectly doable 3.5lb to get off in the bath. As I walked back into the lobby of the Best Western, bang on schedule at 10 a.m., I decided to ask, out of courtesy, what time the checkout was, thinking it would be about 11.30 or 12.

I could not believe it when the receptionist replied that it was in half an hour.

'You've got to be kidding me!' I said, and asked if I'd be able to pay for a later check-out.

'I'm sorry but we're really busy,' she said. 'It's St Leger day.'

'Funnily enough, I know that,' I replied. I decided not to play the card of telling the receptionist I was actually riding in the St Leger, but I don't think she would have known what I was talking about. Perhaps she saw the race on the television that afternoon and recognised me. But if I'd told her I needed the room so badly because

I wanted to sit and sweat in the bath, I'm pretty sure she would have thought I was a complete lunatic.

Anyway, there was no further availability there, and I was going to have to come up with a solution. After a quick Google on my phone, I discovered there was a Nuffield Health Gym near the racecourse. I dashed over there, still in all my heavy sweating gear, bought a day pass and went for a run on the treadmill for half an hour and then a session in the steam room and the jacuzzi. Everything was finally grand and back on track, but it was starting to become one of those days when you wonder what else is going to go wrong.

Harbour Law was a horse I'd ridden a few times before. He had his first run for Jo Crowley at Lingfield that March, when he came second under Sean Levey. Jo had ended up retiring and the owner, Jackie Cornwell, had sent him to Laura Mongan in Epsom. I used to ride quite a bit for Laura. Her husband Ian, who for some reason we all know as 'Jock', was at Gary Moore's before me, and we also used to ride quite a bit of work together at Chris Wall's. There had been some fun nights out in Brighton with him over the years. They put me on Harbour Law when he won on his first start for his new yard at Salisbury, and then we won a Sandown handicap. He was a horse I liked, although not in a million years could I have told you he would win a big one.

Laura and Ian had come up with the plan of going for the Queen's Vase at Royal Ascot, which was then held over two miles. I knew he'd stay very well, so I sat prominently and he finished second behind Colm O'Donoghue on Aidan O'Brien's Sword Fighter, who just kept pulling out a bit more. I felt at the time that Harbour Law had run a great race, but it did gnaw at me a little that Colm probably got a relatively easy lead and could then dictate on his own terms. Knowing how tough my horse became, I do wonder whether I should've been more aggressive on him, and then I might have had another Royal Ascot victory to my name.

It was a bold shout to aim him for the Leger, as he had not had a proper 'prep race', and had not appeared since finishing a close fourth to Housesofparliament in the Bahrain Trophy at the Newmarket July meeting. He had run very, very well in defeat that day, but the ground had been very quick too quick for him, and I felt he wasn't in love with it. Harbour Law had a habit of always leaning to the left in his races, and that was made more severe by the surface. He was quite a chunky, strong animal, and was perhaps looking after himself a bit.

Both Laura and Ian gave me the impression that he was bone idle on the gallops and would only work at the level of the horse you put him with, even though it was obvious he was quite nice. Ten days before the race I was asked by them to ride work on him at Kempton, just with an old lead horse to make sure I thought he was well and moving properly. We gave him a good pipe-opener, and the challenge was on.

Laura and Ian were undoubtedly nervous. It was their first runner in a Classic or even a Group 1, which is a big deal for a small yard with only 20 or 30 horses. Just having a Classic runner is hard, and when you're involved with a horse of such quality you can start convincing yourself that it's going to run very well. I was quite confident, though, not exactly of winning, but I could see no reason why we couldn't be placed, which would be a massive run in itself. We were 22-1 and I certainly thought we would outrun those odds.

They never burdened me with many instructions, but when I'd been studying the form, it looked as if there might not be any pace. Riding a strong stayer, the last thing I wanted was for the race to turn into a sprint, as I knew that would play into the hands of the hot favourite Idaho, a classy middle-distance horse. Having the experience of the Queen's Vase in mind, I told Laura and Ian I would make the running in those circumstances, but it turned out that Muntahaa was very keen with Paul Hanagan, and ended up taking us along flat out. Those are the times when you have to be flexible – if I'd stuck to my original decision to make the running, I would never have won.

I resorted to hold-up tactics instead, sitting out the back, and was in the process of bringing him into the race with three furlongs to go when Idaho stumbled close by and unseated Seamie Heffernan. When you watch the replay, Harbour Law was fighting me the whole way up the straight, and all he wanted to do was lug in behind the other two horses who'd gone clear of the rest, Housesofparliament and Ventura Storm. It was hard work getting him to go upsides the other horses and not just hang in behind.

I knew when I reached Colm O'Donoghue's quarters on Housesofparliament with just half a furlong left that we would win. As soon as we got there, he straightened up and I switched my stick to my right hand. We came just under a length clear, but if he hadn't continually been hanging, we might have won quite a bit more cosily.

Pulling up after the line, Colm came over and shook my hand, and I told him I hoped Seamie was all right, as it had looked a nasty incident. The other jockey I saw very quickly was Paul Hanagan, when I have always got on well with. 'Fuck me Paul,' I said. 'I've just won the fucking St Leger! Can you believe it?'

I guess Paul's horse had not really been expected to be so keen, and the first three had finished so far ahead of the remainder that he'd have had no idea who had finished first. 'Oh, sorry, mate – I didn't realise,' he replied before congratulating me.

The next few minutes were a bit of a blur. I'm never normally speechless – one of my talents is that I've always been good at talking rubbish – but it all just felt bizarre. Firstly I had seen a jockey fall in front of me, and that's never a nice thing to see, and secondly I had just won the biggest race of my career by an absolute mile.

I got through an immediate interview on Channel 4, but as we were being led back off the track, Dan Abraham, a well-known racing photographer, shouted out, 'George, smile.' I guess he wanted a nicer, happier shot than one of me looking as if I was in shock, but he's also one of those characters who often has a bit of banter with the jockeys. As we were walking back and people were clapping and cheering, it became a bit easier to follow Dan's instructions and start enjoying the moment.

When I came back into the weighing room, all the jockeys were waiting just outside the door. The likes of James Doyle and Jamie Spencer were delighted for me, and it was particularly special to see the valets. Two brothers, Robert and Edward Kingsley, had looked after me whenever I was riding up north: they're around the same age as I am, and as a kid I'd stayed with them when I was in their area. Having them sharing in my victory was a thrill, too.

Just before we had returned to the winner's enclosure, it had also suddenly hit me that Nicola was heavily pregnant at home, about to drop at any stage, and that the emotion of the win would have almost certainly sent her into labour. So the first thing I did when I got a spare second to myself in the weighing room was to grab my phone and call her to see if she was all right. Nicola was obviously over the moon for me, but I was not about to become a father at this particular moment. She was just at home, having a fair bit less fun than I was.

I don't even know what I said to Ian and Laura afterwards, or when I collected the traditional cap that jockeys are given as their prize and posed for the photographs. I was also riding in the very next race, a nursery, aboard a horse of the Queen's called Maths Prize. I could hardly take anything in, and I hadn't even had my riding instructions.

I only just managed to get hold of Roger Charlton on the phone before I rode the horse to finish third.

Racing went on until 6 p.m., and I had a couple more rides to get through before driving myself home. It's a journey that would usually take two and a half hours, but it felt like it passed in five minutes, as I spent almost the whole way on the phone catching up with various friends and family.

As much as I'd thought that Harbour Law might run well if a few things went in his favour, to have actually had a result like that started to sink in as being truly amazing. It was not only my achievement but Laura's, as she'd become the first female trainer to win the race in its 240-year history. It was also a huge moment for the once-great Epsom training centre.

To put something of a dampener on celebrations, I couldn't help thinking that the next day I was due to ride at Ffos Las, in what would be a three-hour trek to west Wales. It had apparently rained heavily at the track and of my four booked rides, three had been declared non-runners. All I was left with was one ride in a handicap towards the end of the card for a smaller trainer, Declan Carroll. It would have been so easy to throw a sickie, get home and chill out on that Sunday, but it wasn't my style. I think I'd have felt like a bit of a prima donna if I hadn't bothered going racing, and everyone in the weighing room would be saying, 'He's just won the St Leger – I wonder why he hasn't turned up...?'

So I went down in the car with Dane O'Neill and Frankie McDonald driving, finished third on my one ride, and Dane kindly organised a dinner with some of the guys that night at the Pheasant Inn, a famous racing pub at Shefford Woodlands near Lambourn. Monday evening meetings at Windsor had finished and the rest of the racing was quiet enough, so we could get away with letting our hair down.

Funnily enough, when I went to the Leger as a spectator a year later, I got a lift home from AP McCoy, and I was telling him the story of slogging off to Ffos Las. He said that unless he was absolutely in bits or seriously ill, he'd never jib and would always go racing. One time he'd been due to go up to Sedgefield for one moderate ride for a small trainer, yet he still drove all the way there. If it was good enough for him, it was good enough for me, and perhaps the only similarity I have with AP.

Isabella was born a little while later, in what was yet another incredible sacrifice by Nicola for my career. She was due to be induced on the Friday just before Champions Day at Ascot, where Quest For More was about to run in the Long Distance Cup. As he'd won a Group 1, I thought he had a massive chance, and I told her that I needed to ride him. Nicola was a star, and just got on with it, managing to get the date changed to a little earlier in the week by throwing in a few lies. I think she told them her husband was away on business and she was nervous about being on her own!

It meant I was there for the birth, which was an absolute nightmare. Nicola went in on the Tuesday but was in labour for a day and a half, which was horrific for her, while I was feeling useless and unable to do anything. They gave her an epidural, which stopped working and they had to redo it. She'd have felt everything. It certainly made me glad I'm not a woman.

Isabella was born on the Thursday and we could go home on the Friday. I missed two days of racing, and it sounds so silly to say that I still noticed I'd missed some winners, given that in the grand scheme of things it really didn't matter and I'd got Nicola to move heaven and earth in the first place. Still, I suppose when you're a professional rider you just have that mindset. Quest For More, incidentally, finished second again to Sheikhzayedroad.

Extremely cheekily, and something I imagine I'm still paying Nicola back for now, I ended up leaving her holding the baby – literally – for a week in November when I was invited to take part in a jockey challenge in Barbados. As she couldn't go, I repaid Frankie McDonald for his time at the wheel by taking him along as my 'plus one'. I was out there with Adam Kirby and his partner Megan, Martin Dwyer and his wife and kids, David Probert, Josephine Gordon and Georgia Cox. We had brilliant fun, as we only had to ride on the day after we arrived, and had five more days of holidaying in the Caribbean.

Garrison Savannah, the island's racecourse, is about six furlongs round, and unbelievably tight. I walked the track with Adam Kirby and told him I'd need to have a word with myself to psyche myself up for it. It's quite ridiculous, but all the horses had run round there plenty of times and knew where they were going, so I needn't have worried. Our Britain and Ireland team won every race on the card, and I got one on the board myself.

Guy and I reflected that we'd had a great season in 2016. I'd passed 100 winners for the fourth year in a row and the prize money from the Leger and the Cadran had made it easily my most profitable total.

Soon 2016 became 2017. It was quite a bleak winter, and as normal I was just tipping away, riding for my guys on the all-weather, but by the end of February you start looking forward to the return of the grass racing. Quest For More was due to step up his preparations for running in Dubai, and perhaps I'd be helping out with Roger's future Irish Champion Stakes winner Decorated Knight. He was Andrea Atzeni's ride, but had given me a Group 3 success in the Meld Stakes at Leopardstown that summer when Andrea had been unavailable. All in all, there was plenty to look forward to before I boarded a flight to Switzerland.

CHAPTER ELEVEN
WHITE TURF

If someone offers you the chance of a weekend in St Moritz, you jump at it. The Swiss ski resort welcomes the international jet set during the winter, and for us jockeys there is the White Turf, a short series of race meetings on Sundays, held on the frozen lake at the end of the town. The racing is of only a moderate standard, although the prize money isn't bad, but the main attraction for me was the thought of a good night out afterwards. A few other jockeys had told me that the hospitality and the parties were worth experiencing.

Adam Kirby was supposed to be going to St Moritz to ride for the trainer Jamie Osborne and the Melbourne 10 syndicate, who were sending a few horses across. However, his main trainer Clive Cox had a runner at Wolverhampton on the Saturday night which he would be required for, meaning there would not be enough time for him to get there. Jamie rang me while I was having a game of golf with David Probert to ask if I would stand in for Adam. David had heard it was brilliant fun too, so why not give it a try?

The only person who'd been a bit dubious about the adventure was Joe Fanning, one of the most sensible, father-figure members of the weighing room. 'You're mad,' he said, implying that the racing was something of an acquired taste and not perhaps the safest thing to do.

Saturday's racing didn't go brilliantly. I rode another of Jamie's horses, Battalion, in the Winter Derby at Lingfield, but he sat down in the stalls, missed the break and didn't have the best of runs to finish sixth, before I rounded off the day just getting beaten in a handicap on Etaad. From there it was straight to Heathrow on a flight to Zurich and a two-and-a-half-hour taxi journey through the mountains.

It was only waking up the next morning that I appreciated the beauty of the place. The very swanky hotel I had been put up in had a view all the way to the track, and the stunning scenery of the snow-covered Alps beyond.

From what I could tell from the Swiss racecards, it looked as if all of my four rides had a chance, and when I went down to have a walk on the track, it looked great. John Best, who also had runners there that day and had had a winner when they had staged an extra meeting the previous Friday, had been encouraged about how well it had been riding, too. Although you see snow on the surface of the track, you are, of course, racing on ice underneath and around quite tight bends, which is very different to grass or all-weather tracks. Along with conventional racing, there are some races for locals called 'skijoring', which is where skiers are pulled along by horses. Apparently they can take a fair bit of punishment from bits of ice being kicked back in front of them.

I had ridden my first mount of the afternoon, Boomerang Bob, once before a month or so earlier in a little handicap at Lingfield. Although not exactly a superstar, he was a solid sort of horse, and he seemed fine on the track when we cantered down to the six-furlong start. I noticed that Dougie Costello's horse, who was going along in front of me, was stumbling all over the place, and made a mental note not to follow the horse in the race itself, as it looked like it couldn't pick its feet up.

My biggest concern down at the start was visibility. A lot of jockeys wear ski masks to prevent snow getting in their eyes, but I had brought a more simple face mask to wear with my usual goggles. I fiddled with it to make sure it was on properly and wouldn't make everything steam up.

Jamie hadn't tied me down with instructions, so I took my time towards the rear of the field, and I can remember making progress down the back straight, which is where the lights go out.

What I know from this point on is from other people. Two other horses in the race had come down in front of me, and at the time they thought I had gone over one of the horses on the floor and been brought down. It later turned out that poor Boomerang Bob had gone through the ice independently at a point where there was a weakness in the track. He broke a leg and had to be put down.

It would not have been a pleasant sight for John Best, who had been the first on the scene and raced over to help. Apparently when he got to me I was conscious but wasn't talking. John thought the best thing was to keep speaking to me, so at least it would be a voice I might have recognised, one speaking English rather than French or German. I was staring at him and briefly tried to move, but I wasn't responding to what he or the medics were saying. The lights were on, but there was no one at home. Then John had to go off to a meeting with the organisers to agree to abandon the event.

By the time he came back, I'd been put into an induced coma and my eyes had a bit of tape across them to keep them shut. The chief paramedic told John it was standard practice for the type of injury I'd received, and tried to reassure him that they didn't think I was going to die or anything. Nonetheless, John was very worried, as it was still very serious, and relayed what he found out to Guy, who was passing it on to Nicola.

I was taken by air ambulance to a hospital in Chur, about 50 miles north of St Moritz, where they did a brain scan. News came back across to John an hour or two later that the scan was OK at that stage, and they were going to bring me out of the coma.

From here on, I think it's better that Nicola takes over the story. As you'll discover, when I woke up I certainly wasn't myself, and for the first few days she was the only person to see me.

NICOLA BAKER

Early that Sunday morning George and I 'FaceTimed' each other, and that was when he told me he'd got to St Moritz very late at night. The following week he was meant to be the best man at a wedding, and then we were due to go to Thailand for a holiday – we were leaving on the Tuesday and my mum was having our daughter Bella for a week, so I was rushing around writing lists about spare milk and nappies.

On top of all that I had my best friend's wedding rehearsal to go to that day, and I set off with Bella in the car. I was meant to be there at 11 o'clock, but I arrived 20 minutes early, so I took a walk around the grounds and wrote a message to George. The last one I sent to him just said, 'Are you excited or nervous?' I thought it was a bit weird that I didn't hear anything back.

The others had arrived to start the wedding rehearsal, but about five past eleven Guy Jewell called. It was very strange for him to be in touch with me on a Sunday morning, and when he just said 'Nicola' I could tell from the tone of his voice that George hadn't won a race and something had gone wrong. 'George has had a really bad accident,' he said. 'He's banged his head. They've put him in an induced coma, he's on a ventilator and they're waiting for the air ambulance.'

I had a minute of panic and wondering what I should do, before I said goodbye to my friends, got Bella back in the car and drove home. Mum came over with a bag packed and arrived at about the same time as I did, while Fergus Sweeney rang asking for some medical information for the ambulance, such as, was George allergic to anything? The most difficult thing I had to do was call George's mum and tell her the news. She usually watched all of George's races and thankfully, I think because the St Moritz meeting had been brought forward an hour, they hadn't shown it on TV.

Jamie Osborne and his secretary booked me a flight almost immediately, and I was on a plane to Switzerland by three. There was a car waiting to take me on the hour-and-a-half journey to the hospital in Chur. The most striking thing was that everyone spoke German and not much English, including the taxi driver, and he actually had to take me up to intensive care, as there was no way I'd have found it otherwise.

When a nice nurse took me in to see George, she told me he had been awake and wasn't in a coma any more. It was what she said after that which got me a bit worried. 'If you can wake him up, you'll notice there's something very different about him.'

'George, your wife is here,' she said, and he just grunted and went back to sleep. I could see he had grazes all down his face and a big haematoma, a swelling, on his right leg. They were pure impact injuries, and how he didn't break any bones is beyond me.

The hardest thing is that they gave me a lot of forms to fill out and asked me whether George had a will, and I thought, if they wanted to know that, it must be pretty bad. He was in a ward with four other people; he wasn't on a ventilator any more, but a couple of others were, and it's quite a daunting thing to walk into. It's not just the person you're visiting that affects you: it's the whole scenario.

When I'd got off the plane I'd had a text from Guy saying that George was sitting up, conscious and talking and his CT scan was clear, so it had sounded like pretty good news. But Guy, of course, was only relaying information that had probably been passed through a number of different parties. When I got there, George wasn't up and talking lucidly he was pretty sparko and I started suspecting it could be much worse. The hospital wouldn't tell me anything else about his injuries, and that was when the severity of it all hit me a bit.

I got a taxi to a hotel, my phone going mad with people ringing to see how George was. One amazing thing about him having an accident was realising how many close friends he actually had, who wanted to know how he was, not to gossip or anything, but because they were genuinely concerned. Sam Hitchcott and Pat Cosgrave had even offered to fly from Dubai to Switzerland to be there, and George's phone had literally hundreds of messages on it.

The next day, the Monday, I was up at six to go back to the hospital, and by then George had been moved into his own room. He was in bed for a while and then sat up in a chair – well, more slumped, really – and he was wearing some compression boots fixed to a machine, I presume because they wanted to keep the blood going to the legs.

This was the main trauma hospital for the region, and it was right in the midst of the mountains. I suppose in other circumstances it would have been a lovely place to be staying, and from George's room you looked out to a beautiful snowy scene. When you were sitting there for long periods of time without much happening, it became a highlight when the helicopter came in to land a couple of times a day.

As ridiculous as it sounds, this was the best place ever for an accident to have happened, because they are very used to dealing with injuries like this on the ski slopes. When they suspected a head injury they'd put him into a coma so quickly, so they could control his breathing and protect his brain, and he was transported to hospital safely and rapidly. If it had all happened somewhere else, I dread to think what might have been.

As well as being very, very clean, probably as any Swiss-German institution would be, the hospital was incredibly kind about visiting hours. Technically they should have been two hours in the morning and two in the afternoon, but I was allowed to stay all day. This was also because George had become very agitated – he'd pull at his hair, pull at his scabs, even at the monitors, which ended up having to go on his feet where he couldn't get at them. His suspected spinal injuries meant he also had to wear a collar, but he took that off as well. He'd try to get out of bed and, because his legs weren't working, he'd grab at the handrails. It was a real problem – but when I was there he was a lot calmer. That Monday afternoon they felt it was all becoming a bit dangerous, so they made a cube of mattresses on the floor, and it was safer for him to roll around there. He stayed like that for three days.

George had also been trying to pull out the catheter they'd put in, and they had to take it out in case he caused any more damage. The nurses couldn't get him to use a pot, or understand what he meant when he said he needed a wee. And me trying to explain what he needed in sign language wasn't exactly easy either!

The doctors still seemed to think he was coming around quite well. But despite our initially being told that the CT scan was clear, it seemed there were some marks on it, which were consistent with the type of bruising he had from the fall. He wasn't moving his right leg either, but they thought that was because of the huge haematoma.

On the Tuesday, though, they did a heel prick test: in his right leg George didn't react at all, and even his left arm didn't work very well. By now they knew there was something a lot more wrong than we were hoping. A neurosurgeon came down and said it was either a brain or a spinal injury, and booked him in for an MRI scan on the Friday. They didn't want to sedate him as they wanted to see how the brain was dealing with everything, and doing so might affect its processes of recovery.

In my mind I was turning over which was worse: a brain or a spinal injury? I didn't know then and I still don't. Until this point I'd actually been doing fine dealing with things, but that Tuesday George was a lot less awake, and now I was much more worried. I didn't tell anyone else what I'd been told straight away; instead I called my best friend, who lives in Singapore. I had a massive cry, got it all out, and then I was fine again.

I called George's parents and told them they should come out and see him, and both they and George's sisters and brother came out the next day, the Wednesday. It was as much because I was trying to explain medical terms which I didn't understand down the phone to people who didn't understand them either. The doctors were trying to translate from German to English; it wasn't that good and I was probably only getting half the story. We arranged to have a meeting at the end of the week with all the doctors and specialists.

George hadn't eaten much, but later on Tuesday he got really hungry and then ate in the most extraordinary way. He mixed everything together – steak, mashed potato, orange juice, ice cream – and just put it all in his mouth. That's how jumbled up his mind was. As I understand it, with a brain injury you regress, so maybe this was sort of going back to being a baby. I can tell you what he was eating certainly looked pretty gross.

George couldn't half eat later in the week, though. I had to buy him chocolates from the town, and he hoovered up one of the bars so quickly that as he was putting it into his mouth I was still pulling the wrapper off! He had a big thing for yoghurt too. A lady had come in to give him an injection in his stomach, and she had a yoghurt with her. George missed nothing and very politely asked, 'Do you want me to eat that yoghurt you've got there?' She wasn't sure how he'd even seen it.

Most of the time, though, George was just talking rubbish, and I was desperate to see if there was a little bit of him still there. At the airport I'd bought some magazines to read, and on Wednesday morning I brought them in and pointed to photographs in them and asked him who the people were. He did at least recognise some of them. One of the magazines had Adele on the front cover, and George starting going through this mad singing stage, and belting out 'Hello' at the top of his voice across the entire intensive care ward.

As bizarre as it was, you had to see the funny side. Even the nurses were laughing.

During the next couple of days George went through lots of strange phases. He was allowed to use an iPad to listen to Spotify. When I came back that afternoon he was perched on his hands and knees. I asked him if he was OK. I could see he'd somehow found a YouTube video of bulldogs at an event like Crufts. The iPad was in German, so quite how or why he had chosen to watch this, I will never know, but he had decided to be a dog. Here was something we'd never thought about when giving him the iPad.

The doctors also asked me if I had anything familiar George could hold which might help his progress, and I thought of his phone. We couldn't risk him looking at messages and upsetting himself, or ringing people without knowing what he was saying, so I drained the battery dead and gave it to him. He would just press the keys for hours on end.

But the iPad had a charger, and once when I left him to get a drink – literally for just 12 minutes – he'd charged the phone up with it and managed to call Martin Harley the jockey, who I assume had been the last person to have called George's phone. I rang Guy to ask him to speak to Martin and make sure he kept this to himself, and luckily Martin hadn't spoken to anyone else about it.

Martin had suffered a very bad fall himself at Lingfield a few years earlier, and when George didn't make a lot of sense to him he found it quite upsetting. Martin is quite religious, and so is his father, and his father arranged for George to have a healing blessing. It wasn't possible for George to take the blessing, even over the phone, so Martin's father took it on his behalf, which we greatly appreciated.

We were limiting the updates for the media, both for George's privacy and because we didn't really know much ourselves. There had been some problems with the press, I think mostly in Switzerland – one reporter got through to intensive care posing as my best friend, and saying they wanted to make sure I was OK and ask how George was doing. Luckily the staff came and found me, and I told them there was no way it was my best friend calling. One of the Swiss papers was very, very persistent and the doctors had to hang up on them. From then on, we had a password so that various people including Dr Jerry Hill, the British Horseracing Authority's chief medical adviser, could get in touch.

George's iPad seemed to give him some hidden talents, and for a period on Thursday he decided he would be a rapper. The entire time I had known George I'd never heard him listen to Tupac, or any of that kind of music, but lying on his mattresses he was singing all of the words. Then there was the British artist Stormzy. I don't think George would have even known who Stormzy was – who knows what part of his brain made him search for his music? – but suddenly he was very familiar with Stormzy's work. His sister Zoe was in the room trying to say something, and George said 'Shut up!' in this sort of hip-hop fashion. It turned out that this was just a lyric from one of Stormzy's best-known songs. It's amazing, but so odd, how the brain jumps around like that. George must have heard one of those songs in the past, and it's stored somewhere, even if you don't remember it.

George had a pad of paper to jot things down on, and we could play noughts and crosses on it. Just a game and a half and he was done, and I always had to let him win. He also decided that when he got out he wanted a tattoo, and drew all these ideas out. One was like a clock with Isabella's name coming out of it: he was determined to have it done. Luckily he hasn't turned that idea into a reality.

He had one really nice male nurse called Reinhold. He was the only man in a ward of girls, and although he didn't speak a word of English, for some reason George just clicked with him. Reinhold could move George by himself, and help him to shower and shave, instead of several people struggling with him. On the Thursday afternoon George could talk more, and I came in to find him with Reinhold, pointing at pictures and saying enthusiastically, 'He's got racehorses!', 'This is his daughter!' How, when one man spoke only English and the other only German, they managed to communicate I'll never know, but they understood each other perfectly.

The female nurses had their own issues to worry about with George. The part of his brain that deals with sexual thoughts had been affected, and he became an absolute pest. He asked out every single nurse, and told them that they were all gorgeous. To one sweet nurse called Jessica, a very pretty girl, he said, 'Have you got a boyfriend? When she said yes, he said, 'Do you want another one?' The nurses said it was perfectly normal, and not to get offended, but when you consider that I, his wife, was sitting there the entire time, it's hard not to take it the wrong way.

By Friday afternoon, the results of the MRI scan had come back, and we all had a meeting.

George had had numerous bleeds on the brain, the doctors had discovered, and the reason his right leg wasn't working was because there had been a big bleed on the left side. He was suffering from post-traumatic amnesia (PTA), which is when you're conscious, but in a confused, disoriented state, and the way they measure the severity of a brain injury is by how long you're in that state for. You might never be in it, or just for a little while, but over 24 hours is classed as bad. George would be in it for four weeks.

As well as the numerous bleeds, he had also had what is called a 'shearing' or tearing injury. As far as I can understand, George's fall would have meant that his brain had moved violently backwards and forwards, and the top part of it would have gone over the bottom, damaging the connective parts. While George would know 100 per cent what he wanted to do, said the consultant, he wouldn't always be able to do it, because only 40 per cent of the message was going to the right place. In the future, we were told, if George was lucky, he would be able to walk with sticks.

CHAPTER TWELVE
WAKING UP IN THE WELLINGTON

NICOLA BAKER

The weekend was spent trying to get George home. Organising repatriation is not something you expect to have to do in your life – where to even start? Dr Jerry Hill stepped in again, and was quite amazing. At one stage it looked as if they'd found George a bed in Oxford, but Jerry had been in touch with a great neurosurgeon, Jonathan Bull, who agreed to admit him under his name to the Wellington Hospital in St John's Wood in London, and organised all the finer details.

It was lucky that George had an incredibly comprehensive insurance policy, which included chartered travel. A private jet was arranged, which came from Austria with a neuro-intensive consultant and intensive care nurse on board, but it had to land in Germany instead because it was too icy in Switzerland. They picked us up on the Monday, drove us to the plane in Germany, and we landed at what looked like a military airport on the edge of London. In different circumstances, George might have had to recover in Switzerland for quite some time before he was considered well enough to travel back under medical supervision on an ordinary civilian flight.

The Wellington is a very smart hospital with incredible intensive care rooms, but its visiting policies were far stricter. In Chur I was used to coming and going all the time, but here I wasn't allowed near George, and just had to just sit in the waiting room for as long as it took. Mr Bull, the surgeon, arrived late that night and did a couple of tests on him for hand-eye co-ordination. A major problem was that George now didn't like to wear clothes, and here he was getting really hot and agitated. He was completely naked on the bed. 'We'd better just cover you up a bit, George,' Mr Bull said light-heartedly.

Mr Bull took me outside and said there was no need to operate and that George didn't need to be under his care, so he was passing him over to Dr Richard Greenwood, a consultant neurologist, and we could take it from there. He mentioned other people who'd had similar injuries – he'd talked to Beverley Turner, the wife of James Cracknell, the Olympic rower who was hit by a lorry when he was cycling. George should make a good recovery, Mr Bull believed, but he warned that he would not be the same person, and there were things that would be different. He understood we had a young baby, he said, and one of the things the wives of men who'd experienced brain injuries had found was that their husbands had little patience with their children, because they couldn't control them, and particularly struggled to deal with things if they were loud or unruly.

I stayed overnight in London in a hotel and finally, on the Tuesday, after more than a week away, I went home to see my baby. If it hadn't been for my mum, I don't know what I would have done, as from then on I was back and forth to London every day. She ended up staying for nearly three months to help look after Bella.

After the trouble with the Swiss papers, we made a list of people who were allowed to see George. It was very short to begin with, as he was in such a state, and wouldn't have wanted people to see him looking as bad as he was. Drew Cooney, a very close friend of George's who lives nearer to London, was the only one who saw him in intensive care, maybe two or three days after he landed.

Going into an intensive care ward is not an easy thing for anyone. The Wellington is so sophisticated that we had to wear special colour-co-ordinated gowns to allow us only into particular areas, so there was no chance of cross-contamination. I'd tried to explain to Drew before he came, especially as George did look a real state, but despite the warning he was very affected by it. As well as being hooked up to various pieces of equipment, George looked very limp, and wasn't really able to hold himself up properly.

It was a bit awkward releasing any news to the press, too. There had been one update after his fall, and then nothing for a week, but that was really because while we were waiting for scans there was nothing else to say. I would liaise with the Injured Jockeys Fund every so often to send out a statement, but it would have to be pretty limited. There was obviously a lot of speculation going around, the full range, from him being at death's door to absolutely fine.

Since the accident, I've read quite a few books and articles about brain injuries, from James Cracknell's autobiography to *Where is the Mango Princess?*, a memoir by a woman whose husband's personality changes after a boating accident. But mainly my knowledge came from the brochures and fact sheets provided by the charity Headway.

The worst thing is that no one explains things to you properly. Every brain injury is so different and everyone reacts differently. I mean, is it normal to mush up all your food, or start rapping to music you've never heard before? I couldn't even get to speak to George's consultants on their own. When George was right next to me and thought he was fine, I really couldn't ask them whether it was OK that he was doing something I thought unusual, or tell them I feared something else was clearly wrong with him. The whole thing was scary. How do you get from having known someone for ten years to finding out that those little things about their personality might have changed, or even disappeared? You feel very alone.

I was lucky, however, because Alice Fox-Pitt, the television presenter and former rider, had sent me a message the day after George's accident to say she was there for a chat whenever I wanted. Her husband is the brilliant three-day eventer William Fox-Pitt, who had also had a head injury after a fall. He recovered to ride at the Rio Olympics, but the two of them have been through a lot. Having someone else who had felt the same experiences helped hugely, because no one else really understands.

George was still making good progress, and after a week he was able to move to the acute rehabilitation centre on the other side of the hospital, where he began therapy almost immediately. A problem with PTA is that it affects your short-term memory, so for about three weeks George would repeatedly tell me, 'I've got this really nice therapist, his name's Rob.' I would nod and say, 'Oh, right,' and act as if this was some new information, and then of course Rob, the same therapist I had been seeing come into the room every day, would arrive. That's how confused George was.

They put pictures of the various people he was seeing – the psychologist, occupational therapist, physiotherapist – up on the wall of his room along with their names, so he might start to recognise them. He also had carers 24/7 in the room: they even slept there and took him to the bathroom. He couldn't go anywhere without one as he was so irrational and impulsive; couldn't understand that he couldn't walk and was always falling over or trying to get out of bed. I spent most of the day just telling him to breathe.

Fortunately George showed very little irrational violence, which can be another common symptom, apart from one time about three weeks in when a lovely nurse called Clarence was giving him a shower. George was in a wheelchair and tried to stand up, and when he was told not to he pushed Clarence and they both fell over. George hit his head as well, and had to be rushed off for another CT scan. Thankfully there was no more internal damage, but he does have a little scar on his head as a reminder.

Clarence and another guy called Fred would usually do the late shift, and they were brilliant with George. One time when I came in Fred looked exhausted. 'Hard shift,' he smiled. It turned out he had pushed George around in his wheelchair all night, because he'd been so agitated he couldn't sleep. They'd been all over the floor, going to see the various people around the hospital that George knew. We've been back to see them all again since he left, which was very touching.

George would also try and tip every single member of staff. 'Nicola,' he'd whisper, 'can you give them 50 quid?' I'd explain that either I didn't have any money on me, or we didn't actually have to tip the nurses and porters £50 every time we saw them. I don't know where he thought I'd be getting the money from – he was like one of those millionaire racehorse owners peeling off notes to give to the lads and lasses.

I'd bring in little things from the shops and from home to interest and stimulate George, but the one thing I absolutely regret bringing in is a copy of *What Car?* magazine. George decided straight away he wanted a Tesla, and so every day for about two weeks I'd have to listen to him telling me the same story about them: their battery life, how fast they went, what colours they came in ... Two whole weeks. The worst bit was that when I was driving in to the hospital I would go past this stupid Tesla garage, knowing I had a whole day talking about them ahead of me!

The hospital put an information board up in George's room that spelt out all the important details: 'You're here,' 'This is the date,' and so on, but through much of his period in PTA he'd still have no recollection of time, place or what had happened to him. As far as he was concerned, there was nothing wrong. He'd often say, 'I'd really like to go out for dinner tonight'; obviously you'd have to say no and then he'd get agitated. 'Nicola,' a lovely male intensive-care nurse called Uno told me, 'he's not going to remember this. Just agree with him.'

So when he asked again, I'd say, 'Oh, yes – where would you like to go?' and he'd ask what restaurants were nearby. We might decide that we'd pick an Italian, and I'd tell him I would book a table for 7.30. George would be happy with that, we'd talk about Teslas for a bit, and then he'd say, 'I'd really like to go out for dinner tonight...' and so the circle would begin all over again.

George did know he was a jockey – only too well. He'd constantly say he was riding Quest For More in Dubai, and that we couldn't stop him going there. One time, Dom Elsworth was in the room when five or six of George's rehabilitation team arrived for the weekly meeting. Although George could only just about point properly, he directed a finger at his physiotherapist. 'I'm not happy with this situation here,' he said. 'I'm a very positive person, and in two weeks' time I'm going to Dubai and I will be riding Quest For More. I'm not having any negativity from you, or any of you lot, because that's what I'll be doing.' He was, of course, absolutely serious, and Dom wasn't going to make fun of him. But it was still quite funny to watch half a dozen of the experts standing at the bottom of George's bed nodding along and agreeing with him, when the situation was so ridiculous.

George's consultant would come in twice a week, and he too had already had the conversation about riding in Dubai many times. On one occasion George said, 'You can't stop me: I had my medical last week.' Every jockey has a five-yearly medical, and George had passed his a week before the accident.

'George,' the consultant said calmly, 'you can't walk.'

'Yeah, well, I'll be fine by the weekend.'

'Do you think you can ride a horse?' the consultant asked.

'Well, it might not be pretty,' George said, 'but I could definitely bomb around on it'. He'd never stop.

George was still obsessed with telephones, and was very naughty with them. I had lied at first and told him they didn't work in the hospital, and I urged visitors to keep their mobile phones out of

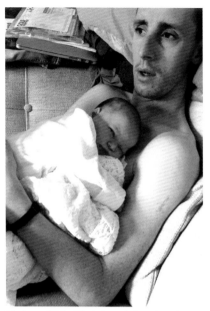

The beautiful, healthy baby Isabella. After a long season and some sleepless nights I was shattered!

Isabella always looks happier with my Mum

Quest For More, an important horse for me, wins the 2016 Lonsdale Cup at York from Pallasator and Oisin Murphy

The highlight of my career. Harbour Law (left) stays on to win the 2016 Ladbrokes St Leger at Doncaster

Celebrations begin as I enter the Doncaster Winners' Enclosure

Some people don't suit wearing hats. As you can see from this weighing room photo, I am not one of those people

A moment that changed my life. February 2017, St Moritz

Swiss Mountain Rescue

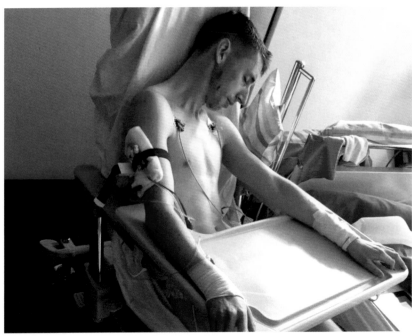

At hospital in Switzerland, and in a bad way

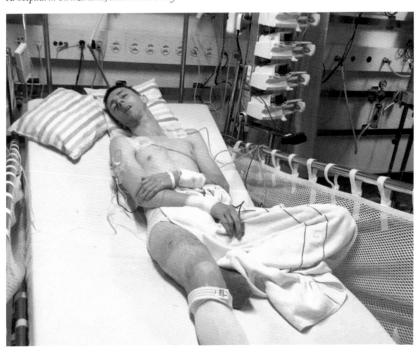

A very, very bad way

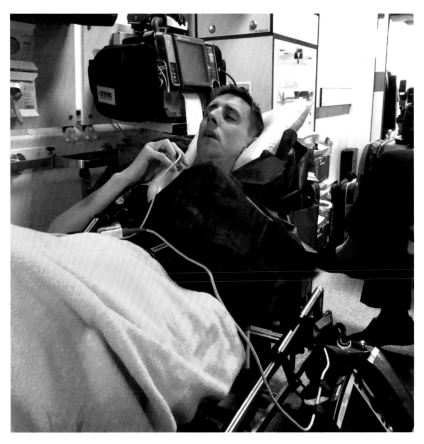

Above: In the ambulance at the start of my journey back to England

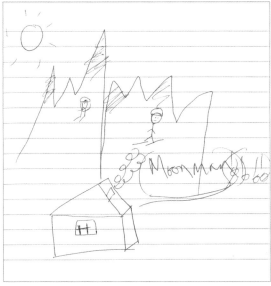

Left: A sketch done in hospital. I don't remember doing it but brain injuries are funny things, they can unlock parts of your personality. For example, I had no idea I was such an accomplished artist

On the road to recovery with Isabella at the Wellington Hospital in London

In rehabilitation at Oaksey house in Lambourn in August 2017

Going beyond the call of duty with Sam Hitchcott (right) at Drew Cooney's (centre) wedding

July 2018, ex-jockeys on tour in Villamoura, Portugal. Richard Hughes (second from right) and I are taller than all of these jump jockeys and yet it was us who rode at nine stone!

One year on from my biggest success in the saddle, I return to the scene at Doncaster, where a new career beckons

Some of the Racing UK team at Royal Ascot, June 2018. From left: Me, Tom Stanley, Britney Eurton and Niall Hannity

sight, because all he wanted to do was call people. If he saw someone with one, he would say something like, 'Can I just check the weather on your phone?' He was desperate to use it. There was a phone in his bedroom, but it was supposed to be disconnected. But one night he called, even though I'd just been to see him. 'Hi, I'm just on my telephone,' he said. 'Anyway, I'm just going to go to bed now. I'll see you later.' The next morning Guy got in touch to say that not only had George called him too, he'd managed to ring Roger Charlton as well. After that, the telephone was removed from the bedroom.

Roger and Guy were both kind enough to talk through their experience with George that night, and here are their recollections.

ROGER CHARLTON

They wanted George's brain and body to recover, so they didn't want him racing forwards too much or stressed, and therefore he wasn't allowed his mobile telephone. The worst thing would have been receiving hundreds of texts all reminding him, 'Oh my God, George, how terrible!'

But one evening at about 10 p.m. the telephone rang, and it was George. 'I'm quite pleased with myself,' he said. 'I looked up your telephone number on Google because I haven't got my mobile.'
I hadn't spoken to him for weeks, so I think I might have said something like, 'George, are you sure? It's you, is it?'

He said, 'I just want to tell you that I might get back in time to ride Questy in the race.'

I thought, well, there was no point in saying no, but it had never struck me as a possibility.

'Well, I'll do my best,' he said, 'because I don't want to let you down, and I think the race will suit, and I think we've got to do this and do that...'

Later on in our conversation he was more saying, 'Actually, I'm really sorry but I don't think I will make it, so who will you get?' and I replied that Jamie Spencer was available.

'That's a good choice,' he said. 'Make sure that what Jamie needs to remember is that he's very slow out of the stalls and wants to challenge wide.' He had it absolutely spot-on as to what I should tell Jamie. He was most concerned, and even offered to ring Jamie himself to explain the tactics...

GUY JEWELL

It was almost like he was drunk when he rang, but he was saying that he had had a bad fall and been lucky, and he was in the right place. He was always searching for new vocabulary as we spoke.

I said to my wife straight away that, as bad as he sounded, I could tell that the real George was in there somewhere. It was really emotional. Although I thought and hoped he was going to be OK, I wasn't burying my head in the sand about the accident – but after that I sort of knew he would be.

NICOLA BAKER

Because of George's antics with the phone, he wouldn't be allowed one for six weeks. It didn't really matter that he'd called Guy or Roger: the problem was, said the consultant, that he might have an hour's conversation with someone and then call them straight back, as he'd have completely forgotten having spoken to them.

I bought George a new iPad as his existing one had all his online banking logins and social media on it. I put all the child locks on it, and it was restricted to allowing him to access maybe ten websites. But he'd want to leave hospital all the time, and was able to call me with the iPad. He'd do this constantly, maybe twenty times, unfortunately, and say, 'I'm getting my bag and getting in a taxi,' and then he'd get emotional, angry or upset when I said no. It's very hard to have the same conversation, trying to reason with someone, over and over again. Eventually we had to restrict him to an hour a day on the iPad.

And while he was hell-bent on leaving we had to sign a Deprivation of Liberty Safeguards document to say that because of his fragile mental state, and for his safety, the hospital could keep him against his will. At least I knew that even when he was telling me he was leaving, and as difficult as it all was, he wasn't going to be able to go anywhere.

Another symptom of the injury was George getting agitated about being hot, because it can cause problems with your temperature. It wasn't that he was actually dripping with sweat or burning up, but in his head he was really hot – mainly, I think, because he wanted to be outside. He's an outdoors person, both in his riding work and going off walking the dogs, and now he found himself shut inside. You can't have open windows in hospitals, especially because people with head injuries are not the most predictable, and he found this very difficult. You wouldn't believe the number of times I had to go off to Oxford Street to buy George a new fan, and then lug it all the way back across London to the hospital.

However, he would always want a better one. They brought a few up to his room, which weren't cold enough, and we even looked at buying portable air conditioning units to see if they were better. It was that much of an issue. Eventually I found a state-of-the-art Dyson fan, which I think cost about 500 quid, and this seemed to make him more comfortable. It was just anything to make him happy.

Another night he had a strop at about 11.30 p.m., after I'd gone home. He FaceTimed me to say he was leaving because his mattress was too hot. I had to call up the nurses, who came and changed it for a very similar one, and apparently this one was colder. The next day I had to buy special bed sheets from John Lewis because the ones he had were really hot. Unfortunately this meant I would have to take them all home myself to wash, because if they went into the hospital system you'd almost certainly never get them back again. We had to get anything that might make him cooler – cold face packs, cold sprays, all sorts of different things.

A big crisis point was that other rooms had a balcony, and George wasn't allowed one. The nurse said they would speak to the consultant and see what they could sort out, but unfortunately there was nothing they could do.

'He's a stupid, stupid consultant,' said George. 'He doesn't know what he's talking about. He doesn't even know me, or what I can and can't do.' The consultant had said no, so that was that, but for a few days George was extremely annoyed.

I felt terrible about the time one of the jockeys who lived near us, Richard Kingscote, came to see George. Richard's wife Ashleigh, who bakes the most amazing cakes, had made a box of them for him. Unfortunately it was the one day George was in the most depressed mood ever. He sat there with his arms crossed throughout and wouldn't speak to us. We'd try to ask how he was doing, and all he'd say was, 'I just want to go home.' It went on for about three hours, with poor Richard sitting there looking and feeling extremely awkward. George even said to Richard, 'You've got to get me out of here,' as though Richard might be able to smuggle him away somehow. It was nothing intended against Richard, so I could only apologise. George was just having a bad day.

George had also been obsessed with the idea that the accident had been his fault. It really played on his mind, and my telling him he wasn't to blame wasn't enough. One day I started getting lots of emails about George requesting PIN changes for his Facebook, Instagram and everything else. It turned out he'd worked out that you could get on to the internet on the television in his room, and had been trying to log on to his social media, which I didn't even know you could do. He also looked up all the articles about his accident. This could have caused him a lot of anguish, but in fact he'd realised that the fall wasn't his fault, and it finally sank in. He was a lot calmer after that.

Four and a half weeks after the accident, George was coming out of PTA and becoming a bit more like his old self. He was less agitated and you could have more of a conversation with him – he'd be more engaged, and asking how Bella was.

As part of his occupational therapy, where they help you to grasp things that bring you back into society, he'd been taken out of the hospital in his wheelchair. They showed him how to cross the road, and pointed out various landmarks, before asking George to find his way back. Understandably, we'd often set off in the opposite direction and get lost. I found it quite an eye-opening experience going out with him when he was in a wheelchair as it makes you appreciate how difficult life is for people who need to use them permanently. It's not only the dips in the pavement and crossing the road: it's how other people walk straight past you and in front of you all of the time.

I'm not sure George had ever cooked for me since I'd known him, but on another occasion in his therapy that's what he had to do. He decided it would be pizza, something he'd helped me make in the past. He had to make a list of what ingredients would be needed and write them down, and then we went to a shop and he got the items from the shelves. He even did a good job of making me some lunch. I should remind him to do it a bit more often!

George's gradual recovery meant that on Mother's Day he was able to see Bella for the first time since he'd left on the morning he went to Lingfield. She wasn't allowed in the hospital, but we were able to go out for the world's fastest recorded lunch in a restaurant down the road. It was pretty lucky that the food arrived very quickly: we were there probably all of ten minutes, which was all George could handle, as everything still made him very, very tired. With all the noise there was just too much to process, and he said he felt as if he was about to explode. But, difficult as it was, it was clearly helpful for him to see Bella again, and since his memory wasn't fully recovered, needing to leave didn't stick with him as a negative experience, or hold him back from wanting to go out again.

A few more people could also start coming in to say hello, from Guy to various other friends and family. Dominic Elsworth was a regular visitor, and in the middle of March, Pat Cosgrave, who had returned from Dubai for a flying visit, was one of his earlier friends to see him. He remarked that whilst George could not really remember what he'd done the day before or who'd been to see him, he still had a surprising recollection of horses and form.

George would often repeat himself, and sometimes you could see how he needed time to process a question and think through his answer. I don't imagine some of the Wellington nurses, just like those in Switzerland, will forget him either, as he was constantly badgering them for dates too. Luckily, as he got back to his old self, this quietened down to just being a bit cheeky with them. Chatting up other girls when your wife is sitting in the room was certainly not going to be permitted forever.

Drew had been brilliant, coming up to the hospital every Thursday to sit for hours with George, I suppose to give me a bit of a break. When the Grand National meeting was on television, they put a pot of coins together and Drew disappeared down to the bookies to put some bets on.

The valet Ian Lawrence, known to everyone as 'Marmite', Willy Twiston-Davies, Shane Kelly and Liam Keniry all came together one day. Willy had just broken his back in a fall and only just been allowed out of hospital, so he certainly shouldn't have been out and about, but he insisted on hobbling his way down on the train. They had asked if they could bring anything, so I told them George particularly loved cake. They had been to a little patisserie and each chosen one they wanted and one extra for George, and we were going to sit and have tea. George hadn't grasped this, however, and just said, 'I don't want the cakes. Put them in the fridge.' I think the lads quite wanted their cake. The next day George ate the lot – six or seven different cakes from strawberry to chocolate – in one go. I took a video of him tucking in and saying how delicious they were, and sent it to Ian.

George had lost a lot of weight, and was down to 8st 9lb, which for his riding career he'd have taken very much as a positive. Nonetheless, the surprising thing to me was finding out how much he loved food. He was eating so much in hospital simply because his body must have been using so much energy to try and heal itself. It made me realise how much self-discipline it must have taken to restrict his eating during nearly 20 years of riding. It was quite incredible.

In particular, it was George's love of chocolate and cake which surprised me. Over the many years of his riding career, he would very rarely have either, or certainly only a minimal amount. To see how much he enjoys eating them now just shows the willpower he must have had to suppress those urges. Because, like most people, when I see chocolate, I just eat it.

Being a jockey means your life revolves totally around racing. So when we became a couple, there were many things we missed out on doing together. There were quite a few occasions, including my best friends' weddings, which I had to go to by myself, because George would either be riding somewhere or be having to do a light weight the next day. It was even those simple occasions when someone would ask if you can do dinner on a certain date in three weeks' time. I'd very often have to decline for George, because he wouldn't know where he'd be riding or what weight he was doing. If he couldn't have dinner, it's pretty miserable going out and watching everyone else eating and drinking when you can't have very much.

Often even Christmas would not be much fun for him. As a family, you sit down to eat things like roast potatoes, Yorkshire pudding and all of the desserts. George could have a bit of meat and some vegetables. He might occasionally have one potato, and that would be it, and skip pudding if he was riding light the next day. That's not a great Christmas, but he knew his options, and knew he couldn't have any more.

In the early years, his weight would be yo-yoing all week, so he'd go out, eat and drink, and be heavy for the first few days. His mood would be very up and down: he'd be short-tempered because he'd be having to sweat so much and was feeling dehydrated and so hungry. Then he'd just about get his weight down, and his mood would probably improve slightly – and then he'd go through the same thing again the following week. It was a real vicious circle.

His mood definitely improved in later years, and he looked better. Instead of not having breakfast and going straight to the bath and trying to sweat, despite not feeling great anyway, he got himself into such a set routine. He was a lot more controlled. It does still seem an unusual regime for someone to have, but it became very normal because his diet was so much better. We'd have a lot of barbecues in the summer, because some barbecued meat and salad was quite a nice and healthy thing to have, even if cake was off the menu.

Further along in George's recovery, the likes of Chris Wall, Ted Durcan, Ed Walker and Roger Charlton's son Harry came in to see him. I was quite taken aback by how many people from racing I didn't even know would offer me places to stay or help, and how many people cared about George. I remember Laurence Bellman, an owner with Ed who lived quite near, said I only had to ask if I wanted his spare room or needed to be driven anywhere. Before George was in the Wellington virtually none of the staff would have known who he was, but they could not believe how popular he was. An incredible amount of cards and flowers continued to arrive to his room.

At the end of March, straight after the Dubai World Cup, Sam Hitchcott came down with me to the hospital, and I know he was apprehensive about seeing George, especially as Drew had been there since the beginning and seen how he'd been in intensive care. As soon as George saw Sam he recognised him straight away, and that they could have a bit of a conversation, seemed a big relief for him: clearly he'd prepared himself for anything. Sam went away to ride at a meeting in China and came back a week later, and told me he was gobsmacked at how much progress George had made in that short space of time, and that he was sure in a few months he would be driving me mad at home again. I suppose, as I was seeing George every day, it was harder to notice the improvement myself.

Other things were easier to measure. By four weeks, and after just four days of being taught with a hoist, and shown how to put your feet down, George was walking. I imagine it was quite upsetting for George's earliest visitors to see him in a wheelchair, them wondering if this was going to be a permanent thing. Seeing him walking again was obviously a relief, but understandably it took time. George shuffled along like one of those cartoon Egyptian mummies, and several people joked with him later that his movement was a bit like a *Thunderbirds* puppet. However, the ward nurse said they couldn't believe how he'd managed to do things in just a few days that it can take many people weeks or months to achieve. It was a massive help that he was fit and light, but also that he's very stubborn and very determined.

CHAPTER THIRTEEN
THE HOSPITAL PASS

GEORGE BAKER

Up to this point in my recovery I've got something of a 'Get out of jail free' card. I remember absolutely nothing of all that weird stuff you'll just have read about me doing; not even a flashback.

There wasn't exactly one morning when I snapped out of PTA and it all made sense. A lot of the early days merge into a blur, and you do also get quite institutionalised. I'd wake up, eat the breakfast I'd ordered the day before, order that day's lunch, dinner and next day's breakfast, before the four sets of therapies would begin, like lessons at school. There might be a few visitors to break up the day. I wasn't thinking about the bigger picture. I was aware of what had happened to me, but it took a while for it to hit home that it was a life-changing thing, because you can't see what's wrong with you. I would have an injection into my stomach every day so I didn't clot up, but I don't remember much other medication. The only physical memento is the scar on my head from falling over in the shower. I knew it would be nice when I could go home, but my one aim was just to get better. The dedication from racing kicked in, and I threw myself into my recuperation programme.

I know it was an enormous relief to the family that some of the old George was coming back, even if I'm sure it would still have been upsetting for them to see me in a wheelchair, and a lot slower at talking. The stage of being hoisted up on a treadmill and being taught how to walk again kind of overlaps the end of my PTA, although I do remember having a visit from Mum and telling her I had something to show her. Holding on to my sister Scarlett for support, I managed four steps one way and four steps back, sending Mum into tears.

Obviously it wasn't always easy. Some evenings I'd be sitting watching TV and I'd feel down, as I would miss my old life. Not just being a jockey, but being normal, and going out and about under my own steam. Then, though, I might see someone moving slowly around the hospital on a frame, or finding it difficult to remember who their family was, and I could understand that though it might be a shit time, in the grand scheme of things it wasn't as bad as what some people were going through. I'm quite realistic like that.

I haven't always had the best experiences with hospitals. Late in 2011 I was riding a horse of Reg Hollinshead's called Flowing Cape, and he fractured a hind leg close to the finish when we were coming through to win a claimer at Wolverhampton. I came off him and fractured my shoulder quite badly, snapping the humerus bone which links to your elbow. There's nothing you can do in that situation: you're down so quickly and unfortunately on the all-weather you don't roll, it just stops you dead.

I got put into an ambulance and knew it was pretty serious. Not only was it fairly obvious it was bust and not looking too good, but it was also extremely painful. As we were driving along, things got more alarming, as I realised I was shaking. I had no idea what was wrong – it was almost as if I was going into shock. Whilst the shoulder hurt, the repercussions shouldn't have been that serious. They stopped the ambulance and it all became clear. The paramedics realised that the ramp they wheel you up on had been left down, and it had been dragging along on the road! When they opened the back door there were scuff marks all the way along the tarmac to the hump-backed bridge where you leave the racecourse. It was more of a relief to me than them, I should imagine.

The hospital in Wolverhampton was not a particularly smart place, and they decided to put a cast on my shoulder because the weight would help move everything back in the right place. When I got home I told Nicola it just didn't feel right – I was in absolute agony. My arm was enormous: it had swollen all around the cast. There was a paramedic who happened to live just across the way from us, and he said we would have to have it cut off straight away.

The specialist I went to see in Reading went mad about what the other hospital had done. He ended up giving me two options: inserting a plate, or going for a process called a palm-tree fixation, where they wrap wire around the bone to pull it together. It would mean I was off for a bit longer to begin with, but wouldn't have to have the plate taken out two years down the line and another six weeks off. Instead they can just knock you out for a few minutes and clip it off.

I was told I'd be off for five or six months, but actually I was back in three. It only meant having the arm in a sling for two or three weeks before I could start to have physio and a lot of rehab in Oaksey House, the Injured Jockeys Fund rehabilitation centre in Lambourn, to build the muscle back up.

Although the Wellington was far nicer than Wolverhampton, and the treatment I received was amazing, you still get cabin fever from being in the same place all the time. I can't tell you how much it got to me that there were balconies in rooms all around the hospital and I couldn't have one. When, finally, and after much persuasion, I was finally given my own, I just loved it. I was still in the wheelchair and wasn't actually allowed out onto the balcony itself, but simply sitting by the open doorway was more than enough. I was in the middle of London, not exactly the cleanest of air, but right then it was as good as being back out on the Ridgeway with the dogs.

At first I wasn't allowed too many distractions, but later on Nicola organised for me to get the *Racing Post* every day. I loved that, and would read it from cover to cover. I'm not sure I was taking it all in, but I was seeing all of the horses I would have been riding and following their results. It didn't matter that I wasn't riding them: it was more that I wanted to see how they were getting on, with a view to riding them the next year. I felt very lucky – as though this was a really big step.

That's not to say I wasn't concentrating on getting back riding as soon as possible. I was still obsessed. I used to think I would be losing all my contacts because I was in hospital, and hope that all the guys I rode regularly for would still look after me when I was ready to return. I thought I'd be back in time for the next Flat season a year later.

Although it wasn't realistic, in hindsight it was still a good thing for me to aim for, as it drove me forward every day and gave me a reason to get out of bed. Without this dream I think it's quite possible I would not have made so much progress, as it meant I pushed myself as hard as I could, even though I was struggling badly with fatigue.

It was only later on that one day I was told exactly what had happened to me. One of the psychologists, Dion Blackler, took me out for a coffee and asked if I minded talking about my situation. I knew I'd had bleeding on the brain, but he explained how it had happened and what it had done. The technical terms, for what it's worth, were a small subarachnoid bleed, a subdural bleed over my left tentorium, a petechial haemorrhage and a shear injury. He told me how it had all contributed to the tiredness, physical problems and strange behaviour. I learned that the shearing injury was as though the brain's wiring was affected, and that it would have to reroute things to other parts of the brain. There was a huge amount of detail about why my co-ordination was affected, and it really helped to understand there was a reason for it all. It made it easier to know what I had to do to get better.

I'd ask questions all the time. How long would things take to improve? When would things start to slow down? The problem is that if you break a bone, you can fix it, do your rehab and get back to normal. With head injuries no one knows what's possible. They know you can get better, but they can't say how much, and as the brain is so complex and all cases are different. But being fit and relatively young, they said, would be important contributory factors in improving.

After a few weeks of being in the Wellington, my progress report would have made far more encouraging reading for my family, even if I was not quite out of the woods. My main goal on admission to the acute neurorehabilitation unit in early March – yes, my main goal – was to be able to walk to the toilet and use it independently, which shows you how much difficulty I was in.

By the end of April I could wash and dry myself when sitting in the shower, was walking better, and had completed various other occupational therapy challenges around St John's Wood. The report read that I was demonstrating 'good insight' into my situation, and was 'grateful for his survival and the positive things in his life', chiefly Nicola and Bella. However, I was still having some issues with concentration, divided attention and occasional impulsivity which they hoped would continue to improve in the coming weeks. Most excitingly of all, it suggested that returning home, with limited requirements for care and specialist equipment, was somewhere on the horizon.

First, though, it was going to be possible to move me much closer to home, to a neurorehabilitation unit at a hospital in Salisbury. From there I would have to prove I was safe enough to be allowed out for good. I spent two months in the Wellington and was told I could expect to be in Salisbury for another two months. It felt as if it was the final major test: be a goody two-shoes for a while and then you're out.

The reality was very different. I got home an awful lot sooner, but only because I suffered some of my truly darkest moments. There were a lot of very ill people in the dependency ward where I was placed in Salisbury. And while there was nothing wrong with my treatment, or the hospital itself, where I had my own room, it was the troubles of others which began to affect me.

In the Wellington I hadn't been around people who were too agitated, perhaps partly because of luck, but also because I hadn't appreciated quite what a dog's bollocks hospital it was. In Salisbury, there was a lot of shouting in the night and I was struggling to get any sleep. One guy nearby was a double amputee who had lost both legs – I think he'd been in the Army. Whatever it was that had happened to him, he wasn't right mentally at all. From what I could hear he'd seem to be doing OK during the day, but then at night when no one was with him he would kick off.

I suppose I was coming along quite well – I could go and pick up my own breakfast, in so far as I could pour a cup of tea and take some cereal. The Army guy was in the breakfast room one morning too and, although I had never even met him before, he thought I was his son. It was so weird. Head injuries are a horrific thing to deal with, truly horrific, and his was clearly so much worse than mine. When you see someone in that much pain, it's always going to leave a scar, but if I'd seen him when I was 100 per cent well myself, it would have been easier to deal with and eventually put it to the back of my mind and not worry about it.

In another room next door there was also a lady who didn't know where she was, and would cry all night. I feel selfish now for saying how much it ground me down. But it also made me realise that I wasn't better either. When I arrived in Salisbury I kept wondering what I was doing in that ward, because I wasn't that ill. At times I thought the same thing in London, too, but inside I kind of understood that I obviously must have been ill to be in there. In Salisbury it plagued me that there was no way that I should have been in that part of the hospital, because it was for Looney Tunes.

Now I can look back on the experience with a clear mind, I still know I shouldn't have been in that ward. When they had applied to move me to another hospital, I possibly did need to be in a behavioural unit, but by the time I physically left the Wellington I'd improved so much that I probably didn't. It seemed to take time for me to be reassessed in Salisbury and for the wheels to be put in motion.

To begin with there was also no therapy because we'd moved over a bank holiday, and there was no one in my room any more to keep an eye on me or guide me along if I needed to go to the loo in the middle of the night. Having had a busy schedule and people to talk to all those weeks in the Wellington, I think I also began to feel lonely.

I suppose having a bit of freedom and just sitting in my room was OK for a little while, as I caught up on all of the TV I'd missed. To start with I was also sympathetic to what the other guys around the hospital were going through. As time went on, though – even within a couple of days – I really started going on a downwards spiral. The lack of sleep was having a major impact on my mood and wellbeing. I had no idea how long it was going to be before I could move somewhere quieter, and began to think, 'If this is where I'm going to be stuck, I don't know what I'm going to do...' I'd always felt so positive before and wanted to get better, but now I was shutting down on myself. I almost got to the point where I wondered what I was trying to get better for. It was that bad.

Nicola came every day and could take me out for dinner. A visit to Pizza Express in Salisbury went down particularly well, as it was the first time I'd been to a restaurant properly again. Food would always cheer me up, but when Nicola was dropping me back I felt like a prisoner being sent back inside after day release. As Nicola took me back down to the ward I was walking so slowly she would almost have to drag me along the corridor. I'd become quite teary and emotional. For my own safety and security I wouldn't have been allowed to leave by my own will, so it felt as if I was locked in. Nicola became very concerned that I was actually going backwards and had numerous worried conversations with Lisa Hancock, the Chief Executive of the Injured Jockeys Fund.

I'd been there less than a week before I could take no more. Nicola had just left and it all started kicking off again. It was so *noisy*. She was nearly back to the house when I rang her up, bawling my eyes out. 'I'm going to go mental here,' I said. 'If you don't come back and get me I'm going to have to get a taxi and come home.'

You'll know we've been there before with me wanting to check out, but this was different. Nicola turned the car around and we went to speak to someone at the hospital. It turned out there was an empty bungalow on the site which would be an option for me to stay at, and they mentioned the possibility of letting me go home for the weekend to straighten myself out a little before coming back to the hospital next week. But by now it was lodged in my head that there was no way I was staying in this place another night, and Nicola knew that if she let me come with her for the weekend, there was no way she'd be able to get me in the car to come back. We spoke to the guys at the Injured Jockeys Fund, who'd been providing assistance, and everyone eventually came to a decision that I'd be allowed to go home a month or two earlier than I should have been.

Nicola stayed the night in the bungalow with me and then, at the end of April, we left, never to return again. When I'd left London to go to Salisbury I'd been feeling really positive and delighted, only for the sensation to fade away. But on the way back to my house, I've never been as elated in my life.

I'm sure it would have been fine, over time, if I had returned to that bungalow. The truth was, though, that I felt the place had already done me some damage mentally. It had seemed like I was in hell. Physically I was still improving, but I was in such a bad frame of mind, and rest had been so important in determining how I felt.

I've had many sessions with Dr Ben Papps, a clinical neuro-psychologist at the Hobbs Rehabilitation centre in Winchester, and it actually took a long time to get over this period in Salisbury. One of the main issues concerned the Army guy. I used to think about how he was going to be in there every night, and how things just shouldn't be like that. Then there was the lady who didn't know why she was in hospital and cried all night. I felt so very sorry for them, and it really affected me knowing that they would still be struggling along in there.

It was only in December 2017, seven months after leaving hospital, that through these sessions I felt I'd overcome those demons, an experience I'd never had before. As much as they were shit circumstances, I suppose being there did also make me very resilient. It's horrific when you're actually there, and you think that you're not going to get out the other side, but when you do it makes you a stronger person. It almost defines you as an individual.

Oaksey House could help with my ongoing treatment, and some jockeys also go and stay there full-time to recuperate. Unfortunately, the site is not watched all the time, and I couldn't be allowed there at night on my own, so I needed to stay under Nicola's supervision instead. I don't think I would have done anything silly, but you never know. I could have bumped into a friend and gone to get a Coke or something for a catch-up, but have ended up in a busy pub instead, and that would not have been the best thing for me. But I could still go there every weekday to continue with all of my therapies. As cliched as it sounds, there was a light at the end of the tunnel.

CHAPTER FOURTEEN
COMING HOME

There were obviously struggles when I first got back home. Having had to guide me through every stage of my recovery this far, Nicola was now into even more unknown territory. Clearly I needed regular prompting and supervision, but at times I would get frustrated because I thought Nicola was over-mothering me and telling me what to do too much. I didn't like to feel I was being patronised, and it was hard to appreciate that it was just her caring and making sure I was sensible, rather than any bossiness on her part.

There had been a plan to go and live at Nicola's parents' house in Newbury for a while, where I'd have been able to have a downstairs bedroom, but everything had happened in such a rush that at first we had to go back to our three-floor townhouse.

The first morning I got out of bed and when I got to the top of the stairs and there was a whiteboard. Written in massive letters were the words, DO NOT GO DOWN THE STAIRS ON YOUR OWN. I had to try to be a good patient and do what I was told, even if I wanted to shout, 'For God's sake, I'm 34 years old!' I knew inside that I had to go down on my bum for my own safety, or get Nicola to help me along, but over time you get fed up with taking orders and feel that you're better than you are.

It was really, really hard for both of us. In all honesty, I shouldn't have been out of hospital care so prematurely, and we also had a six-month-old child added into the equation. I'm sure an occupational therapist would have had a field day around the house explaining where we should have put handles on the walls, while going back to getting in a normal shower was something Nicola had to assist with. The problem was that I had self-discharged from Salisbury, against medical advice, so there was no obligation to provide us with any services.

I took the middle floor and Bella and Nicola were upstairs, but I would often have huge problems sleeping, almost nightmares at times. We'd have to move our rooms around, putting Bella on her own and me going in with Nicola. When I was in Salisbury I'd stopped taking any medication to calm me down, because it had been discretionary and, as I have explained earlier, I still thought I was fine and didn't need it. There were other times when Bella would be crying for an hour and a half solid, and I would just be fast asleep and not hear a thing.

Nicola admitted to me later that she'd wondered if she'd done the wrong thing in allowing me home, as she didn't know what she was dealing with at all. Luckily, Oaksey House also shared some facilities with a branch of Hobbs Rehabilitation, which provides specialist treatment for brain and spinal injuries, and I could be enrolled to go in there every day, too. But for the few days before everything was set up, Nicola had to do the therapy with me. The day after I'd been set free we went to a retail park in Newbury and bought tennis rackets and balls. Out in the garden, Nicola would throw balls in different directions and angles and I would try to catch them.

We'd take the dogs and Bella off for a walk and Nicola would make me do little obstacle courses, such as jumping onto logs and hopping up and down. There were so many silly little things I needed to learn how to do again. Even getting out of a car was awkward, and it took me a long time to master it again.

Nicola was so fantastic at kidding me along. Most of the other people in my ward at the Wellington had suffered head injuries from cycling accidents, and one of the legacies of being in there was that I was adamant I would never ride a bike again; it was too dangerous. Nicola got a bike out of the shed one afternoon and began riding it around the garden. She decided to use the tactic of, 'I bet you can't ride a bike,' a reliable way of playing to the stubborn side of my personality, and she got me back on it, if only to prove her wrong.

Nicola was right about the stairs, of course. I couldn't go down them unaided without looking at my feet, because I would always worry that I'd fall over. One of the first things I was asked to do at Oaksey House was to hold a piece of foam in my arms, so I couldn't see my feet or hold on to the rail, and then walk down the stairs.

The physiotherapist, Rob Treviss, had devised loads of little tests to improve my co-ordination, sensory awareness and fitness, such as putting random numbers from one to ten on the walls and calling them out, and I would have to touch them with either my left or right hand.

Of course, you don't feel you're slow at this sort of stuff when you're actually doing it. It was the same in London, where a big thing was that they timed you doing everything, even simple tasks like walking a circuit around the ward. If you're a few seconds quicker at something after a couple of weeks, it really helps to know that you're making an improvement, even if you can't recognise it yourself.

Hobbs Rehabilitation helped me to set goals for my first few weeks at home. When you feel a bit ill-prepared to be released back into the big wide world you can become anxious, so the targets were always realistic, starting off with going to the newsagent on my own to get the paper, helping with household chores and walking the dogs. I would have other things I would have to try out and build on, such as getting used to talking to larger groups of people again, or becoming more confident about pushing Bella in the pram. Sudden changes in plan would be harder to deal with, but as long as I knew where I was going and what I was doing, I was comfortable.

I wore one of those Fitbits, which monitor and track your activity, and was given the task of doing 10,000 steps a day. First it was a private battle with myself and then, as Nicola and various other members of the family were wearing them and they were all linked up, I had to beat them too. If I was a bit behind anyone towards the end of the day, I'd have to go off for another walk in the evening just to get myself back ahead. That sense of competition clearly never leaves you.

Sometimes I'd still be in my own little world. A month after I'd left hospital I went to get my eyes tested, as head injuries can affect your eyesight, and straining your eyes can make you feel tired. Nicola was pretty specific with her instructions: I should go into the opticians and then meet her for lunch half an hour later in Camp Hopson, quite a well-known department store in Newbury. Although I did actually need some very weak glasses, from the opticians you can literally see Camp Hopson opposite.

After 40 minutes, Nicola rang me. 'Where are you?'

'I'm just in John Lewis,' I replied.

'Why are you in John Lewis?'

'Because we're having lunch.'

I'd already been to Marks & Spencer and wondered why Nicola wasn't there. I think basically I'd got distracted, as when I left the opticians it had begun to rain, and I'd gone into the other shops nearby to shelter. I'd been told by Nicola to always use the lift, but it had been quite liberating to be out and about on my own, so I disobeyed her. You wouldn't ever think it could be quite exciting to go on an escalator, but it was.

Three and a half months after my accident, I went to the races again for the first time. My trainer friend Ed Walker drove me down to Goodwood for what, as far as I was concerned, was a dry run for Royal Ascot. Well, it probably was a dry run in the eyes of the people around me, who had seen me when I was really bad, but I knew I was going to Royal Ascot no matter what.

The expedition didn't exactly start off in the best of fashion because I hadn't brought any accreditation with me so they wouldn't let me in! In the old days I would usually go in through the back entrance with my gear, and the staff would know who I was, so Ed had to get hold of an owner's badge from the front desk. I hadn't brought a tie with me either, disobeying the racecourse dress code, and they just about let me off that one.

Ed had been well briefed by Nicola, and was careful not to rush around too much. He left me outside the weighing room for a while to catch up with old friends.

He survived the experience of keeping an eye on me for most of the afternoon, but I must have tested his patience at one point when we walked outside to watch a race from the front of the stands. Ed and Bjorn Nielsen were running a filly that they quite fancied, and two furlongs from home, just as she was looking to be going well and Ed was starting to get a bit nervous, I turned to him and said, 'Well done – you've got this.' My race-reading judgement was obviously taking its time to return to normal, as the filly swiftly got beaten.

Going to Goodwood was about proving that I was OK being on my feet for a longer period of time, while my brain also had to deal with all of the sensations of being out and about amongst more people. Although we'd chosen a quiet and low-key afternoon, at a race meeting there are always lots of sights and distractions. One consequence of the accident I would struggle with – indeed, am still having to manage – is eliminating background sound. Imagine yourself at a dinner party, for example, where there are three or four conversations going on around you at the same time. I'd be trying to follow one, but unable to shut out the others, and feel I was in a blur. It would make me very tired. I've always been bad at concentrating as far back as school, so I suppose the accident has only made it worse.

I did make it to Royal Ascot, both for Gold Cup day on the Thursday and later on the Saturday. Bjorn Nielsen had a private box, and it was perfect the way they had arranged it: just Bjorn and his girlfriend, Nicola and the Charltons. I only had to worry about people I knew, and it wasn't packed and disorientating like it would have been in the stands or in a restaurant. When it came to the Gold Cup itself, Roger insisted I came down with him to the paddock to see Quest For More. I was very sceptical: I felt a bit out of place, and there were the long escalators and the steps down to the weighing room to negotiate.

Not riding that day didn't feel weird, but the strange part was that Quest For More and Harbour Law were both running in the same race. I was standing there looking at the two horses who had played such massive parts in my career, and although I hadn't yet made any sort of announcements about whether I was going to come back, inside I was thinking, 'I wonder if I'm ever going to be able to ride them again?'

Perhaps I looked a bit awkward, because the next thing I knew, Nicola had tapped me on the shoulder and said, 'At least you didn't have to choose which one you were going to ride.' It was one of those little things which helped to lighten the moment.

I didn't see the Harbour Law guys in the paddock, but Jamie Spencer was riding Questy and Roger, in a really cool way, told me to give Jamie his orders. I'm sure they would have discussed things already, but it was a thoughtful gesture. I don't know which one I actually would have chosen, and it turned out that Harbour Law ran a blinder in third, but Questy didn't show his old form and was later retired.

There were other daunting outings up ahead. I'd got to know Drew Cooney from my days in Hungerford, as he had grown up with Sam Hitchcott in East Grinstead and they'd remained very close. He's not a racing man at all, but was friendly with a few of the jockeys. Drew had gone beyond the call of duty in coming to see me so frequently in hospital, not to mention being such a huge help to Nicola, and we had a bit of a private pact that I would do my best to make it to his wedding to his fiancée Gemma in Italy in early July.

I don't think in a million years he would have thought I'd make it there, having seen me early on in intensive care in the Wellington. When I'd been in hospital he'd provided some pictures of my wedding, and all the good times we'd shared in the past, I guess to spur me along. No promises were ever made, but I worked my arse off to be fit enough to take a plane to Italy and down to Sorrento, the beautiful town on the Amalfi Coast where we stayed for a few days. It was a big step, and if I'd had the money I'm sure I would have gone on a private jet, but Nicola organised everything to make it as easy as possible for me. We even went to Luton Airport the night before the flight so it wouldn't be too long a day.

We did learn a few things for the next time, as I got a bit stressed at the check-in, just because the airport was really busy and I didn't like queuing for anything. Nicola ended up looking like a camel, carrying all the luggage and our wedding suits, while I just carried my phone, which I tended to be obsessed with. I wouldn't even wear a backpack, as I complained it was too heavy and would make me tired.

Then, for some reason known only to myself, I decided I wanted to put my toothbrush through the security machine individually. Unfortunately the toothbrush rolled off the belt and fell out of its box. Because I also had a phobia about cleanliness, this caused a great deal of shouting and swearing, with Nicola telling me to please calm down. We sat and ate breakfast in silence, and travelled on the plane without speaking another word as I sulked about a toothbrush.

Perhaps, along with paying for speedy boarding, fast-track and the lounge, I'm just better off travelling on planes without Nicola at all!

I was an usher at the wedding, and even had to wear a kilt during the ceremony on a very warm day. It clearly meant a lot to Drew, who mentioned Nicola and myself in his speech. I couldn't start drinking, or going along with all the activities, but our hotel was within walking distance, and at about nine o'clock I left Nicola to it and slipped away to bed.

It was great to see friends like Rab Havlin and Sam in happier surroundings. Since the Hungerford days, Sam and I have always remained very close. One afternoon we sat on the sun loungers and chatted for hours like old times. I think Sam was relieved that he had the opportunity to do this with me again.

We have a history of taking the mickey out of each other. Sam's a big Everton fan, and we had an acquaintance who every so often would get us tickets for a match at Goodison Park. I'm not much of a football fan myself, but would enjoy playing completely dumb about it, asking whether Everton were the team in blue, and various other idiotic questions to wind Sam up just as he began to get more and more engrossed in the game.

But in Sorrento it was Sam who was taking the mickey out of me, owing to my dubious choice of footwear.

Nicola and I had decided to walk the ten minutes or so from our hotel to the town to meet a few of our friends for a drink. I had it in my head that my flip-flops were rubbing, and so Nicola knelt down and put some cream between my toes. Maybe she put a bit too much on, because then I thought I was sliding around, and I hated not feeling stable. I told everyone that I was going to find some new ones, and returned ten minutes later with a pair of 'Jesus sandals'.

'These are so nice!' I enthused, which caused a fair bit of ribbing, especially with my skinny white legs surrounded by all these huge straps.

Frankly, as long as I was comfortable, I didn't care what I looked like. I just loved those sandals, and wore them all the time on the holiday. I suspect Nicola decided to draw the line at me continuing to wear them back home as they seemed to mysteriously disappear from our travelling luggage.

Getting me to wear a kilt had been something of a challenge, as my fashion sense had taken a downward direction. To start with I would only wear Crocs clogs when I was at home, inside and outside, before graduating to trainers. Then I got an obsession with jogging bottoms, and Nicola would have to put up with me wearing them everywhere, from when we were out having dinner to a meeting with a consultant or the accountant. Shorts, too – I'd find a pair I liked and then buy three more pairs in different colours. Then I'd decide that I didn't like the pockets of that design, and order four more of another type.

I'd come out of hospital at 8st 12lb, and for a while remained very skinny before I started putting weight on again, so this involved an awful lot of clothes buying. There are four pairs of so many different items in our wardrobe that we could probably open our own shop, if not a particularly stylish one.

Obviously going away to Italy was a huge personal achievement, even if Nicola was there to hold my hand. I was also starting to be able to go to a few places on my own again. That July I'd been invited to present the trophy for Newbury's Super Sprint, and during lunch I'd been seated next to Ciaran O'Brien, who is the communications director at the bookmakers William Hill. He asked if I fancied doing some work for the company, and I said I'd love to, not really thinking that anything would come of it.

First thing on Monday morning Ciaran rang me and asked if I would help with some promotion of the St Leger, of which they'd just taken over the sponsorship – to be an ambassador at a lunch in September to launch the race. With my future as a rider pretty uncertain, it was an exciting opportunity to do something different, and proof that you've just got to get out there and put yourself about, because you never know who you might bump into. I could easily have decided to stay at home that Saturday, and would never have met Ciaran.

The lunch was not only my first time back in London, but it also meant getting a train on my own. I remember Nicola dropping me off at the station and looking absolutely terrified. I think she thought I might end up anywhere, and she told me firmly to get a taxi to the hotel at the other end, but I was confident enough to go on the Tube and get there under my own steam. All the little steps feel like you have gone forward a mile.

Physically I looked OK – perhaps a little unsteady on my feet and a bit pale – but people who didn't know me wouldn't have seen anything wrong. I gave the press and the guests a rough outline of my progress, and expressed my hopes of riding again, explaining that it was going to be a long journey back but I wasn't ruling anything out. I nearly tipped the winner too, picking Stradivarius partly out of loyalty to Bjorn Nielsen: he ended up running a cracker to finish a half-length third to Capri.

I did some corporate work for Hills on the actual day of the Leger, meeting and greeting and doing various interviews, and hopefully this is something I will continue to help them with in the future. Later they asked me onto their table for the Horserace Writers' and Photographers' Association awards in London, which was certainly an occasion where I had to be sensible and go home early, given that the drinking seemed to have started even before lunch.

During the early sessions with my psychologist, Ben Papps, I'd discussed with him how I might get back to riding if I ever got the medical all-clear. I was still hoping the miracle was going to happen, and whenever anyone asked if I was going to come back, I would say, 'Who knows what's possible?' But it was only when I was settling into a routine back home that it started to dawn that it was going to be a harder thing to do than I'd thought. Alice Fox-Pitt had said to Nicola that when William had first started riding again, no one could see him doing it, because he had his own stables and riding facilities down at their home in Dorset. I wouldn't have that option. If I'd gone down to Roger's and had a go at proving myself on a racehorse, everyone would have seen me struggling and been talking about it. My balance is so bad, it would have been horrific to watch, and most probably I'd have fallen off.

So I created an imaginary 'William Fox-Pitt Island' in my mind, where Ben and I would go on the gallops and no-one would see me practising. This never became a reality, but I guess it helped me to visualise my situation and think about it more deeply. I didn't really speak to anyone apart from the psychologist about my doubts, but as time passed I was aware how hard everything was. I could feel it in day-to-day things, just getting around and getting on with life, that physically I just wasn't the same person.

What finally made me realise that riding wasn't going to be possible was when, towards the end of that summer, I watched a documentary called *The Crash Reel*. It's about a superstar American snowboarder called Kevin Pearce who was about to start his qualification for the 2010 Winter Olympics, only to have a fall from which he suffered a severe head injury. It was a fairly shocking thing to see Kevin after the accident. Once he was getting better, he didn't feel – very much like I did – that he was that bad. He went and talked to a specialist about wanting to be a professional snowboarder again. And for me, even though I hadn't yet talked to the doctors, that's when it started to sink in.

Kevin would tell his family he didn't care what they said: he was going to snowboard again. There was a big comeback sequence, where all his friends and family went down on the snow together, but the problem was that Kevin wasn't very good any more. Later, he went to see other snowboarders who'd had significant brain injuries and remained seriously unwell, and his own situation began to dawn on him. Nowadays he has his own foundation for people who find themselves in a similar position, and does lots of public speaking.

The moment that affected me most was when Kevin was telling one guy in hospital to keep being positive. When he walked away he told his mother how glad he was that he hadn't been in the same state when he'd had his accident. She replied that that was exactly what he'd been like. Just like me, Kevin had no concept of how he appeared through the eyes of others. It was the same thing: your family being really concerned, and yet you don't care. We both thought we were fine. Looking at Kevin was like looking in the mirror.

I got a little emotional during the documentary as everything was hitting home. I ended up watching it over and over again, a bit like the footage of my St Leger win. I suppose I was wondering if I'd missed anything, if perhaps somewhere in it there was a bit of hope.

Weirdly, when I looked back through my messages from the early days after my accident I found one from Nathan Horrocks, a former jockey who now runs a successful equine film production company, suggesting that watching *The Crash Reel* would really help. I'd forgotten all about it. It turned out that Nicola had bumped into Nathan subsequently and he'd mentioned it to her again. So she'd watched it herself, but had waited until the time was right to mention it. I think if I'd watched it too early it would not have had the same impact: I wouldn't have been particularly bothered, and just seen it as a problem someone else was having to deal with.

I needed to have goals, and if you're knocked down too much, it's easy to give up. Looking back, I think it was pretty clear from a medical point of view fairly early on that it wasn't going to be possible for me to return to riding, but no one wanted to burst my bubble, as the prospect was such a driving force in my recovery.

Whilst Nicola was not forcing me into any decisions about what I was going to do, she could probably tell that I was now a bit more open-minded about possible scenarios. I think I shut myself in the living room a couple of times, but I never remember feeling despondent or wondering how I'd be able to carry on. I just needed a bit of time to myself to gather my thoughts. Nicola was able to talk to me, and telling me how the situation had felt to her made something really click with me.

By now the family had moved back to Newbury, and I'd gained more independence, in that I could walk to the gym myself and play tennis. This gave me a purpose. After watching *The Crash Reel* I was talking to Ben once a week, and I said to him that even if I couldn't be a jockey any more, I was still going to attack things and do everything I could for my fitness to get back to as normal a life as I could possibly have. I even went through a stage of weighing myself again. As Nicola saw me trundling down to the gym every morning, I had a sneaking suspicion she thought I was lying to her. 'This bastard is saying one thing,' I imagine she thought, 'but he's still trying his best to get back riding.'

But I was just trying to help myself to get better in any way I could. I never quite gave up on my dream, but I had accepted things. The documentary had made me realise that being a jockey again would not be possible. Ben really helped me to deal with letting go, and I've never seen anyone look more relieved than Nicola when we finally talked it all through.

Nicola had also read me extracts from James Cracknell's book. At the end of each chapter, his wife describes things from her point of view. It was quite hard to listen to. James thought what he was doing was normal, but Beverley was seeing it all differently. The similarities with Nicola and myself were uncanny.

It was a really strange time for us. I was going to a few race meetings, doing a few talks in corporate boxes, but it wasn't just the stress of getting me ready that Nicola disliked. I'd get stopped by so many well-meaning people asking me how I was doing, and with Nicola right next to me I'd always reply that I'd be back riding before long. I imagine she was always wondering what on earth was going to come out of my mouth next. I had a useful response which I could call up like pressing a button. 'I don't know what's medically possible at the moment,' I'd say. I've no idea how many times I must have said it, but I reckon I've uttered that sentence more than any other in my life. At least no one questions what's medically possible: it was like saying it was out of my hands. But Nicola knew that I might still forget I'd spoken to someone even earlier the same day, so it was hard for her to just play along and agree when people said, 'Isn't George amazing, he's back to his old self!' As I began to feel better and better, I could see Nicola was still worried about me.

In late October, around the end of the Flat season, I finally went to see Dr Jerry Hill of the BHA to discuss my future. I told him about *The Crash Reel* and asked him if I was wrong about my case.

Jerry had visited me twice in hospital, and I'm sure he'd have found it quite concerning to hear me talk about Teslas and Land Rover Discoveries for two solid hours. He'd also seen me later when I was out of PTA and doing an awful lot better, and sat in on some consultations, so he had a very good idea of the situation. He said it was a good thing I had accepted I wouldn't ride again, rather than have come to see him expecting to get my licence back and have to be let down or told to wait another two years and try again. It was a chat I hadn't been looking forward to, and although there's always that hope against hope, deep down I knew what the answer was going to be. Balance is everything on a horse and I just wouldn't have been safe on one. More important still was if I ever had another fall, which would most likely involve hitting my head: no specialist would know how my brain would react, and for that reason alone, I wasn't going to get a licence.

Soon after seeing Jerry I rang Paul Struthers, the chief executive of the Professional Jockeys Association, and told him I would officially be retiring, but asked him to keep the news to himself for the time being. Actually admitting it to someone, formally, felt very final, and I did get a bit emotional. We were in the car on the way to Oaksey House at the time, and I asked Nicola if she could pull over. I opened the glove box, picked out a banana, and said, 'I think I'm going to eat this because it's going to make me feel better.' Nicola just collapsed in helpless laughter. It was the hardest thing I had had to say to anyone the whole way through, but I still felt a kind of relief. We'd be OK.

I hadn't actually told my parents yet, and very quietly Paul set some of the wheels in motion. I did an interview with Alastair Down for the *Racing Post* about my decision. The *Racing Post* were very discreet and said they would hold on to the story until I was ready to go public.

I wanted to bow out in the right way, on my own terms, and so in early November I spoke to all of my trainers and everyone close to me before making an appearance on *Get In!*, a light-hearted show on the At The Races channel with the former jockeys Luke Harvey and Jason Weaver, both of whom I got on well with. I was sort of OK with it by now, and held it together as I told them it was important for me not to dwell on things, and to try and move on with my life. While I was appearing live on television, the Injured Jockeys Fund released a statement on my behalf:

> I had a very bad accident this year and suffered a serious head injury. Whilst my recovery is going well, I have been thinking about the future and, in consultation with Dr Jerry Hill at the BHA, have accepted it is not medically possible for me to come back to race riding.
>
> Since my accident, my wife Nicola and family have been incredibly strong, and their positivity has made it so much easier for me to get through the bad times. The Professional Jockeys Association, The Injured Jockeys Fund and Oaksey House have looked after me, and I'm well aware that if it wasn't for their help, I wouldn't be as far forward as I am. I would like to thank all of them so much, as well as the wider racing community for their support and incredible kindness.
>
> I have not decided what my future holds, but I will continue with my recovery programme and get as well as I can.
>
> Although I will not be able to race ride again, I consider myself extremely fortunate to be where I am now.

CHAPTER FIFTEEN
A SLIGHTLY CHANGED MAN

It's been said by friends that I will never realise how much Nicola has done for me during my recovery. Some of this I'm not able to understand or remember, but I'd like her to know that I will always appreciate it.

Nicola stood by me through thick and thin, and never faltered once. She was so very strong, and I can never really thank her enough. It's hard to put into words what she went through; and in a way she suffered more than I did, because it's only Nicola who has the memories of all of those terrible early times. No matter how much the specialists prepare you for the future, it would still have been very strange. We'd been together for quite a long time, but not a really long time, and Nicola had to adapt from being married to a man who had been very independent to one who was completely helpless.

I do know that it's not just the stress of worrying about and looking after Bella and me that she's been through. When you have an accident such as mine there are so many things you haven't considered, first and foremost money. We didn't have a joint bank account, and so Nicola had no control of our finances. She had a little bit in her current account, and mine had enough in it to cover a few payments, but neither lasted very long, and more money would need to be transferred around. In the beginning Nicola used one of our credit cards, but unfortunately as soon as she went to the bank and asked about moving some money to another account, they cancelled all my cards! Even though Nicola was a director of the business, they wouldn't even talk to her. In the end, she had to get power of attorney, because I was obviously not in a sound mental state to be in charge of anything.

We were also in the middle of selling our house, which was in my name, so poor Nicola had no legal right to sign anything. When she was in Switzerland she couldn't even make international calls from her mobile, because again that plan was under my name and she didn't know the pin number. She ended up having to speak to doctors via WhatsApp. The insurance companies were also not interested in talking until Nicola had the legal authorisation to do so. It was all quite a rigmarole.

When I was just out of PTA, someone from the council came to the Wellington to interview me to ensure I wasn't being financially exploited. I had to answer a heap of questions like, 'Do you trust your wife to be in charge of your bank accounts?' and, 'Was the house on the market before you had the accident?' If my wife was to start doing anything strange, such as moving away or buying things that I didn't think she should be buying, I could call them up and they would withdraw her power of attorney, which in any case only lasted for a few months. I suppose incidents like that do happen, with relatives or partners of someone who's not fully aware of what's going on robbing them blind and disappearing. Luckily they didn't ask why there was a £500 fan on the latest credit card statement!

Before the accident, we had been trying to buy another house in a small village outside Newbury but it turned out to be a blessing in disguise that the sale fell through. As pretty as it was, it would have been much more isolated than living in town, and I would have been far more reliant on other people to get anywhere, because driving, or the inability to do so, was perhaps the most significant obstacle placed in my path during the later stages of my recovery.

The DVLA had seen the report from the specialists about my injury and revoked my licence, and it's quite hard to get it back, because they want to know that you're OK to drive again. When I was in hospital Dr Greenwood, my consultant, told me he was sure I would be more than able to drive again, but he couldn't sign me off, as they have to see proof that you're safe on the road when you're actually put at the wheel of a car. The reason I didn't have a licence any more was because my cognitive speed had been quite badly affected. This is basically your awareness of what's going on around you while you're driving – like noticing other cars stopping for pedestrians crossing the road – rather than a question of how well you can handle the car.

Around April 2018 I had to go up to Birmingham to undertake an off-road assessment. It was the first time I'd been behind the wheel for more than a year, and I felt a bit naked. It was really quite weird, but luckily we were in a very quiet neighbourhood, and I must have done well as I was given a provisional licence, which meant going back to having to use the dreaded 'L' plates. As soon as I was eligible, I went to Oxford for an actual assessment. I probably overdid the preparation and had loads of lessons, as though I was a learner once again. I was pretty convinced that they would want to know I'd been doing a lot of practising. The thought of being able to get out and about for the day-to-day stuff – going to the races and seeing the likes of Roger Charlton and Ed Walker at their stables, made all the red tape and waiting worth it.

Doing a driving test as a teenager is one of the most nerve-wracking challenges, but in my favour, I suppose, was that as a jockey I had been fairly good under pressure. Important as it was, I knew I had to be relaxed, because if you're tense, you always make stupid mistakes. This was just another hurdle to jump. I was always pretty confident I would get this particular licence back in the end.

Awareness is fairly crucial in driving, and I'm not sure mine will ever be perfect. If it has returned as much as it ever will, then great, but there's always the hope it will get even better. Like most men, I'm not saying I was ever mega at multitasking, but it is a lot harder now. If I was on my phone and something else was happening in the same room, I would struggle to take both things in. For similar reasons,

I haven't yet been allowed to look after Bella on my own. This is on partly mental, partly physical grounds. Certainly, there would be a worry about what could happen if I were to get distracted and she did something silly, but a bigger issue is my balance. If, for example, she was messing about and I had to pick her up, or stop her from grabbing something, it's when I'm rushing that I struggle. When I have enough time to think, 'I've got to pick Bella up,' I can do it just like any other father. It's precisely those 'worst-case scenarios' that are the problem – if I fell over with her or something.

I've had to try to look at it rationally and not get frustrated. The best way to accept it is knowing that it's just another step in the process of getting better, like getting my driving licence back. I understand that people aren't being horrible; they just want my daughter to be safe. If you over-assess it, it'll drive you mental. I know I can look after my daughter, but I have to do the best by her. And it'll change. I've been able to ease back in slowly, taking Bella out for walks in the pushchair, and it'll build up from there. At some stage Nicola will be more confident in giving me more responsibility.

I still can't skip, either, as I discovered at Christmas when my little niece Edie tried to teach me. Skipping is hard enough anyway, but without great balance and co-ordination, it is fair to say that Uncle George made a bit of a fool of himself.

It's obviously much harder for Nicola than me to come to terms with the fact that, while many aspects of the man she married have now returned, there are still little things which are different. I used to be quite easy-going about everything, but now if, for example, I can't find something I'm looking for, I might flip, and it becomes a massive deal. I'm gradually becoming more relaxed, but can still have moments when I'm not rational about things, and it's a matter of my way or the highway.

Nicola still has to check that I'm getting things done – documents, emails and things that need organising. She feels that 75% of the time she doesn't need to, but there's still that other 25%. Just over a year after the accident we were going to the Cheltenham Festival, and I'd left my suit jacket in the wrong car. She asked me if I'd got everything, and suddenly I wondered where my jacket was. If she hadn't reminded me, we'd probably have left without it! Another time I was getting the Eurostar to Paris with Bjorn Nielsen and Roger Charlton to see a horse run, and they picked me up in the car to go down to London. It hadn't even entered my mind to bring my passport, and if Bjorn hadn't asked everyone to double-check, I'd have got all the way to St Pancras and not been allowed on the train. It was one of those silly, embarrassing things which in the past I'd have instantly known, or looked up beforehand.

I'm also even more OCD about cleanliness than I was before. This became fairly major when I was in hospital, and Nicola believes it went back to the time I had been asking about seeing Bella. The real reason she wasn't allowed in the hospital was because they want it to be a good experience when you see your daughter for the first time again, so we went out of the hospital for that brief Mother's Day lunch together. I think to appease me at the time, one of the doctors or nurses said it wasn't good for babies to be in the hospital because of the risk of germs, and I became obsessed with this idea. So everything had to be sanitised, and when I was in the wheelchair I took antiseptic wipes out with me. When we were in the park I'd even take my jumper off before holding Bella in case it had been contaminated. When we got home I also told Nicola she should throw that Dyson fan away because of the hospital germs. Sensibly, given how much it cost, she refused, and I think she pretended that she had changed its filter when I insisted that this was the least we should do.

I'm not quite such a Howard Hughes these days, but I do like to have some hand sanitiser gel on me. I think this germ phobia is also what made me refuse to go into any of the swimming or hydro pools, from the Wellington all the way to Oaksey House and even the shallow pool at our holiday hotel in Italy for Drew's wedding. For a long time I was adamant that I would not go swimming, but many months down the line I finally popped into the pool at the gym when Nicola was teaching Bella to start swimming.

I've managed to conquer many of the smaller things. Admittedly, I decided to have the luxury of travelling business class, with the lounge and the greater likelihood of getting some sleep, but in early 2018 I still proved my independence by taking a flight on my own to Dubai. I stayed with the jockeys Pat Dobbs and Pat Cosgrave for a few days, and although we couldn't exactly go out clubbing every night, we played loads of golf and went to quieter places for dinner. My only mistake was to go shopping for suits during a stage when I was still skinny, only to find a few months later that they were welded to me.

Tennis has been a lifesaver, too. When I was first going into Oaksey House, they said I needed to find a hobby for therapy. One day we went up the road to the house of John Francome, the legendary jump jockey, who is a patron of the Injured Jockeys Fund. John is a keen tennis player who has his own court, and I found I enjoyed just knocking the ball around. My movement was terrible, but I seemed to feel better, and I caught the bug. I had some lessons at the club in my gym, and joined the beginners' and intermediate leagues. I suppose at first it was more about taking me out of the house every day, finding a way of filling time and getting into a routine. It would also help with fitness and co-ordination, but another benefit is that I've made a new group of friends in the area. I'm something of a novelty for some of the, shall we say, slightly older, ladies who make up quite a lot of the leagues. Tennis probably helps even more because it's a game I hadn't played much at all before the accident, so I can definitely see I'm better than I was when I started.

Golf is still my main sport, though. Perhaps I'd have been playing a lot more of it if I had a golf course rather than a tennis court at the end of my road, but it has proved more frustrating. I'm simply not as good as I was. At first I had to get a buggy everywhere because I struggled with walking, and sometimes I'd come back from the course in quite a negative frame of mind.

Maybe I just need to play better. At least having had lessons and essentially starting again has meant I don't have any bad habits. Trevor Rogers and Billy Nicholson, a couple of guys I know from racing, were very kind in taking me to a local course and helping me with the clubs, just to get me out and about for a couple of hours.

It was a special moment when I played my first round since the accident, as it was with my old golfing buddy Dom Elsworth. When he first came to visit me he'd left the Wellington in tears, I was in such a bad way, and it had looked as though it might take me years and years to have any sort of normal life again. He'd tried to get to the Wellington at least once a week, and had also been one of the few people to have seen how miserable it was when I was trapped in that ward in Salisbury. We had just teed off on the first hole at West Berks and were going down the fairway when Dom turned to me and said, 'George, if someone had said to me less than six months ago that I'd be playing golf with you now, I'd have never, ever, ever believed it.'

Dom had suffered an injury himself when he was concussed in a fall at Ffos Las in 2009 and had some bruising on the brain. It affected his balance, and at one stage his riding future was very much in doubt. After more than a year on the sidelines, and no shortage of determination, he returned to the saddle, and towards the end of his career had a good association with Henrietta Knight. Now we had ended up playing together on a charity golf day organised by the former trainer Jim Old. Also on our team was the racehorse owner Bryan Mathieson, who had spent a long time getting back on his feet after a stroke, so together the three of us had a fair bit of experience recovering from head and brain injuries.

In the early days after I left hospital, Dom was very considerate about breaking up the monotony when I wasn't busy. Now he's retired from riding he works for a company supplying pharmaceuticals to the veterinary industry, and sometimes if he was heading to Newmarket he'd take me along so I got out of the house and saw some familiar faces. He's discreet and a good listener, and whilst our injuries were quite different, there were some similarities. When I talked about the prospect of riding again – Dom and I have always talked a lot – he told me to remember I wasn't under any pressure to say or do anything. I was better off just taking my time and seeing how things went. Sometimes, he felt, sportspeople announce their retirement a bit too soon, and find themselves sinking into depression.

Luckily the changes which have happened to me really only affect my domestic routine. As for racing, I'm fortunate to remember everything that I did, and I continue to soak up the form and everything that's going on. I'm sure I would be allowed to sit on Premio Loco or another quiet horse again if I really wanted, but it's not something I've been desperate to do. It's not the same as riding in a race, and that chapter of my life has closed. I don't look back at my career with any regret or bitterness. Obviously it would have been nice to have won more Group 1s, but it was lovely to win a Classic, and that was definitely a box I wanted to tick. My accident would have been much harder to take if I'd been younger and not had the time to prove myself. One day at Oaksey House I met Ryan Hatch, the young jump jockey who had to retire prematurely because he was at risk of a serious spinal injury. I'm sure he'll be fine in life, and he has some Cheltenham Festival winners to look back on, but I'm sure he would have had many more ambitions in the saddle which he can't now achieve.

I still love horses or racing, and I just have to do something else connected with the sport. Frankly, I'd be a waste of time doing anything else. I'm open to offers, and I wouldn't rule anything out in the future. Once I actually applied for a job, for the first time in my entire life. My CV was a little on the short side. But after what I went through, I'd just like to make sure I don't tie myself to anything I don't enjoy doing.

No sooner had I announced my retirement on At The Races, however, than things snowballed. The other racing channel, Racing UK, asked me on to one of their shows, and they helped me forge a new career as a pundit, along with the odd guest appearance on ITV. It wasn't something I'd thought seriously about doing, I didn't chase it, and it became another unexpected and interesting journey.

When the trainer Martin Bosley said to me, years and years ago now, 'Ride for as long as you can, because when you pack up you've got to work for a living,' I didn't really take it in. He was absolutely right, however: riding was far easier. Television requires a lot more homework, but I hope my insight is beneficial and a bit different. It's enabled me to start looking to the future.

In the grand scheme of things, I'd take how well I've come out of this all day long. When I try to walk backwards, or in a different direction, it's hard, and sometimes doesn't feel like me, but I've learned not to get frustrated. This is how it is, I know: it's a work in progress and hopefully things might keep improving. One specialist I saw said that they had dealt with people in my position for a long time, and that often five years down the line something small will suddenly get better. It might not seem like a big thing to everyone else, but to you it will feel like an enormous achievement.

I don't always feel I've come a long way, but whenever I watch a video of myself early on in the Wellington, it really makes me realise that I have. When, a few weeks after the accident, what had happened to me started to sink in, if someone had said to me that I would be feeling so much better in myself, indeed normal again, only a year later, I'd have thought they were joking.

It wasn't even just from that time at the hospital. Someone showed me a clip of an interview I did on television from the first time I went back racing at Goodwood. I looked like a ghost. Now I look so much healthier. It's an ongoing process, though, and you've got to be realistic. With head injuries people can get depressed if things don't go right, so with work it was important to ease myself into it gradually.

Way back, during my time in the Wellington, Dr Greenwood told me that the most important therapy I would ever have would come from my psychologist, and that I would continue to see them for a long time afterwards, maybe even for the rest of my life. I do. The psychologists tell you to keep your head right, and it's important to talk about your feelings. At the time it was a massive thing for me to start opening up more, and there was probably still an element of putting on an act, just as I had done as a jockey. You'll always make out that you're all right, rather than actually saying what's wrong with you.

I still see Ben Papps to make sure I'm still progressing, and the topics we discuss are wide-ranging, running from personal issues to preparing for starting to work again – basically steering you in the right direction. But it really helps to speak to anyone. Just talking with Tom Peacock through the various stages of my life for this book has been useful, too, and I'm sure that I'm far more candid than I have allowed myself to be in the past.

It used to really annoy Nicola when I'd say, 'There's nothing wrong with me.'

'George,' she'd reply, 'you are not the same person — don't kid yourself.'

It's true, but I'm always looking for the positives. I'm very lucky that my speech and my memory are pretty good now, and if you met me and hadn't known me from before, you'd probably only notice that I do walk a bit like a *Thunderbirds* puppet. I was told to try and swing my arms a bit more while I was walking so that I didn't look quite so wooden. Perhaps one day I'll have a new career as a catwalk model.

In my old routine I had to be strict with myself, and the new routine has required it too. I still have to take myself off early if I do anything in the evening, and steer clear of alcohol, as it's not worth compromising my recovery. Normally if someone tried to put you to bed at ten, or stopped you from having a drink, you'd say 'Bugger off and leave me alone.' But I've had to treat myself, unfortunately, as a not-very-well person who can't afford to go out burning the candle at both ends. The truth of it, whether you've had a head injury or not, of course, is that when you're having a good night out you always crave more.

I'm all right about everything now. Thanks to the help of a lot of people I'm in the process of getting better, and this is my story so far. My ongoing recovery has been like riding in another race, really. Don't be in a rush. Time's a massive healer.

ACKNOWLEDGEMENTS

You never know what life is going to throw at you. When the shit hit the fan in mine a whole team came together to help me through it all, centred on my unflappable wife Nicola. She supported me through all my 'lost' time as well as looking after our baby daughter, Isabella. She is the voice of reason when I need it. She was, and is, my rock.

Thanks also to my family: my parents Peter and Tracie, and my brother and sisters, Zac, Zoe and Scarlett. My in-laws Penny and Stuart Dumelow were so generous in letting us live with them for almost a year.

From the scene of the accident, I owe a huge debt of gratitude to all the medical staff who cared for me at the racecourse and at the trauma unit in Chur in Switzerland. I also want to give due credit to my fellow jockey Kieren Fox, who rode a horse for John Best in the fateful race, and helped gather my possessions. He went above the call of duty, by all accounts, and later helped with the research for this book.

I thank the Professional Jockeys Association and the Injured Jockeys Fund and their staff, especially Paul Struthers, and Dr Jerry Hill of the British Horseracing Authority, who was instrumental in getting me to the Wellington Hospital. In London, it was the staff of the Wellington, under the supervision of my consultant Dr Richard Greenwood, who set me on the path to recovery. I am also very grateful to Danny Charlesworth and his son Greg, as their company Citipost sponsored me for many years and continued to do so after my accident, which they were not obliged to do.

When someone's in their time of need the world of racing does come together amazingly well, and I was taken aback by the support I received. I can't name all of you who came to visit me while I was in hospital and sent me messages, but your words of encouragement and good wishes were much appreciated. You all know who you are.

My recovery continued at Oaksey House, run by the Injured Jockeys Fund, and the staff of Hobbs Rehabilitation. A special thanks must go to Rob Treviss at Oaksey House who really helped my physical recovery, and kept pushing me when I needed it. Also to Ben Papps of Hobbs, who is continuing to work with me on my recovery back to normal life.

George Baker

TRIBUTES

TOM PEACOCK

Decency is the quality that shines through in George Baker. He was unfailingly helpful and considerate in our sessions together, as well as self-deprecating, interesting and, most of all, honest. It was hardly a surprise, given what a popular jockey he was, and one can only be impressed by his triumph over adversity. I think both George and I got a lot out of working through a story which others will hopefully find just as moving and inspirational.

To help with events and descriptions during the writing, and to view George through the eyes of others, I spoke to quite a few of the people who know him best. This book simply would not have worked without Nicola's insight, along with additional help from George's parents Peter and Tracie, and his friends Sam Hitchcott and Drew Cooney in particular.

I was struck by how, largely unprompted, so many would point to George's good character. George would be too modest to want to include anything, but I believe the tributes that follow only add to what you should have already learned about him.

ROGER CHARLTON

Everybody always says what a nice person George is. He's quite a good role model: he sets a good example for other people. We've got a few apprentice jockeys here, and I've told them he's the sort of person who would watch their rides and help them, much better than someone like me, who isn't a jockey, having them in and asking them why they did something. George watches racing avidly, he's canny, and would tell them when they should have done something differently. He'd help them as if they were his own children.

I don't really know how he came to start with me. I think it was because he was local and wanted to come and ride out, and then he progressed. George and I never had a retainer: just an understanding. You have to have loyalty between trainer and jockey, and George was always deeply respectful of that. Considering his size, which is pretty unique, George was very professional in how he wasted and looked after himself. I don't think there was ever a question of rushing things: he was very disciplined. I don't think I ever had a cross word with him about anything, or him with me.

He always thought things through, and his opinions were always well worth respecting. If he said a horse he was riding wanted seven furlongs or shouldn't run at a certain racecourse you felt pretty confident in his judgement. Having that kind of guidance is always very helpful.

He's very understated, but he has a great chuckle and a good sense of humour, without being noisy. I thinks he helps people a lot. If jockeys tap on his door and tell him their problems, I think he'd give more good advice than most people. In that regard he's 'm'learned friend'.

It must be horrible when things like he's had to face up to start to dawn on you, but George has been so mature. He knows he has a wonderful wife and child, he's lucky to be alive, and he's happy, not frustrated, about what happened. It shows the depth of him.

GUY JEWELL

As an agent, you're used to trainers complaining that a jockey was rude or grumpy, but that was never the case with George. His PR skills were something else. In our 13 years together I can't remember a cross word between us – George might have barked at me once, I might've barked once at George, but that's it.

I can't believe how level he remained, even when he was starving. The person nearest you is always the first person to get it, but he never, ever gave me a hard time because he was having a hard time. Given what he had to do, that is amazing. He not only has a very positive personality: he has an absolute iron will.

If anything, now, we're just really good friends rather than former colleagues. Our families are intertwined – I'm like an old bit of ivy: I'm in there now.

MARK USHER

A very important side to George is that he had such a determined streak inside him to make it, but the second thing is that he was just a pleasant guy to have around the place. He had to have the chances, but he created his own environment to succeed. And he was certainly not a spoilt kid, with his father and mother always working hard, and learning from people like Dermid Hyde before he joined me.

I think all that helped him to overcome the adversity he had in his career, because he always had the talent. He had a very good empathy with horses, and felt able to articulate what he was thinking to owners, which was a big help to me.

JOHN BEST

I always say that if I could have had any jockey as my number one, George would have been it. If he'd been a jockey able to do 8st 7lb instead of over 9st, I think he would have been champion time and time again, or riding for someone like Coolmore or Godolphin.

He is one of the most intelligent and talented jockeys I have ever seen riding. If I couldn't get George for a runner and my jockey

wasn't sure what they wanted to do, I'd say, if you see George in front of you, make sure you're up there with him, because it'll mean you're not going fast enough. If he's out the back, make sure you're not going forward, because it will mean you're going too fast. For me he was the best.

PAT COSGRAVE

He's just a nice guy, George. He was quite sensible, because he had to be, and all-round good at what he was doing and concentrating on his racing. He had a very good racing brain, very good tactically and at dropping horses in so they could finish well. Most of the time he'd be behind you, but not usually at the finish.

It would take a lot to upset him, but if you did, you'd know about it. The only time I ever did was when I kicked his ball off the green for a laugh when we were playing golf one day. He went mad at me!

I still speak to him about things race-wise. He's very good at looking in at racing from the outside now, coming at things from a different angle. It gets tougher when you're older with the weight, but he rode a Classic winner, which not many people will do, and he's retired with a new chapter ahead.

ED WALKER

We all wish George was still a jockey, but he's an immense help to us now, just in a different way. He gets what the game is about. He's one of the most intelligent jockeys I've seen riding, and that stands him in great stead for the next stage of his career.

I spoke to Nicola a lot over the weeks and months, and she has been a tower of strength. It's a shame that his best era as a jockey was his last, but George knows that there's no point in dwelling on what might have been. He's amazingly positive, never feeling sorry for himself or regretting things. I'm sure he still has tough times, as everyone does, but he feels blessed for what he has and that he's back in good shape.

MARTIN HARLEY

He's a very brave man, both as a person and a rider. He was never afraid to take a risk on a good horse, and most of the time he got it right. Particularly with the weight problems he had, the amazing thing was that he was always cheerful and joking around in the weighing room. He was a great man to have around.

DOMINIC ELSWORTH

George's and my head injuries were very different, but George was very good to me when I was off. He came round and broke my day up for me when he wasn't riding. He'd take me to places and be encouraging, and I've tried to be the same with him. Just being a mate, really.

If you've got a pot on your arm, a pot on your leg or you're using crutches, everyone knows you've got an ailment, but a head injury is a very grey area. He's still got a long way to go, but he'll get there, and his dry sense of humour has always helped him to get through things.

What's amazed me is that he's been so logical and meticulous about it, but that was him before: it's what made him such a good jockey. In getting hold of his weight, he had structure to his life, and he's added that same structure to his rehabilitation and getting better.

GARY MOORE

He was a top-class rider – only the weight meant that he didn't reach the heights he would have done otherwise – and he's a top-class person with it. You knew where you were going with horses when you talked to him; his feedback was always so good and so helpful.

You don't need to give riders like George orders. He gave me orders, really. It wasn't easy to get him in the end, because people had latched on to how good he was. I'm amazed how many winners he rode for me in such a short space of time.

CHRIS WALL

If we ever sat down to dinner, I would often say after I had eaten three lettuce leaves that it was about as much as George would get to eat all week.

He had everything you would look for in a jockey: able to get a horse to settle, good hands and a well-delivered challenge. He would never hurry horses, and although you knew jolly well that on occasions it wouldn't work, he was always man enough to say what he had done wrong and wouldn't blame anyone else. He took everything seriously. He won a lot more races that he shouldn't have done than lost races that he needn't have done.

It was hard seeing him in hospital, when it was more like he was steam-driven than being of the digital age, but he has come out the other side.

The fact that George wanted to have Premio Loco when he retired because he felt that he owed the horse sums him up as a person. I'm proud to call him a friend.

INDEX

All photographs copyright George Baker except for:
Plates 1   Page 2 (bottom left) Martin Lynch
             Page 5 (top) Edward Whitaker/Racing Post
             Page 6 (bottom) Edward Whitaker/Racing Post
             Page 7 (top and bottom) Edward Whitaker/Racing Post
             Page 8 (top) Edward Whitaker/Racing Post

Plates 2   Page 1 (bottom) Edward Whitaker/Racing Post
             Page 2 (top) Edward Whitaker/Racing Post, (bottom left) Anna Gowthorpe/PA Wire
             Page 3 (top) Liesl King, (bottom) Andy Mettler
             Page 7 (top left) Edward Whitaker/Racing Post
             Page 8 (top) Edward Whitaker/Racing Post, (bottom) Tom Stanley